W9-DIJ-155

WITHDRAWN

THE SOLO TRAVELER'S HANDBOOK
2nd Edition

For those who love and those who long to go solo.

Janice Leith Waugh

HUNTINGTON CITY TOWNSHIP
PUBLIC LIBRARY
255 WEST PARK DRIVE
HUNTINGTON, IN 46750

The Solo Traveler's Handbook: For those who love and those who long to go solo

© Copyright 2012 by Janice Waugh

ISBN 978-0-9877061-2-6

All rights reserved. No part of this publication may be reproduced, stored in or introduced into a retrieval system, or transmitted in any form or by any means (electronic, mechanical, photocopying, recording or otherwise), without the prior written permission of both the copyright owner(s) and the above publisher of the book.

ISBN 978-0-9877061-2-6

Cataloguing data available from Library and Archives Canada

Disclaimer:

This book provides entertaining and informative snapshots of the writer's personal experiences and helpful tips from the writer and others, learned while traveling around the world. The tips provided in this book are not meant to serve as an exclusive checklist to effectively safeguard the reader in every travel situation. Each reader should complete updated, detailed research from legitimate sources to learn the cultural norms and safety recommendations for their specific destination. No one can guarantee safety and travel can expose everyone to potential risks. Because safety is impacted by each person's actions and choices, each reader is advised to always do their homework on their destination and use their best judgment while on their journey.

I wish you safe and happy solo travels.

For my mother,
whose independent streak has been
an inspiration my entire life.

For my four sons
of whom I am very proud
and with whom I share the loss of Ron.

For my sister, Karen Dale Egan,
who has supported me in countless ways
on the journey that is the Solo Traveler Project.

Acknowledgements

Oh my goodness, how can I thank all the wonderful people who have helped me with the 1st and now 2nd editions of The Solo Traveler's Handbook. My thanks first go to my trusted readers who gently tore my first draft apart, Dale Egan, Elizabeth Verwey and Jeff Jung. Then to The Travelers Handbooks authors who supported the idea of a series with their own books and then encouraged me to expand my own. They are Jeff Jung, Jodi Ettenberg, Shannon O'Donnell and Sarah and Terry Lee. Thank you to Simon Constam whose critique and support has improved this book immensely. Thank you to my proofreader and Associate Editor of Solo Traveler, Tracey Nesbitt and to the book's designer, Ana Botelho. Thank you to Joe Yonan, Bruce Poon Tip and Bella DePaulo for taking the time to read and review my book. Thanks to Allen Bullard, Stephanie Phillips, Jodi Ettenberg, Sean Parry, Jane Okpala, Saralee R. Leary, James Steel, Keith Jenkins, and Kathy for contributing their solo travel stories and perspectives. And, of course, thank you to my sons, mom and my entire extended family who have supported me with this book and the entire Solo Traveler project.

Contents

Contents

Contents

Introduction to the 2nd Edition

A 2nd Edition so soon?

I know. It was just last year that *The Solo Traveler's Handbook* was published. How much could have changed? Well, I've traveled a lot since then and I have more tales to tell and tips to share. But there's more.

The Solo Traveler's Handbook has spawned a series. A collective of travel writers has formed and more handbooks for other styles of travel have been written. We now have a series called *The Traveler's Handbooks*.

My original handbook was the model for the other books in the series but, as would be expected, the other authors improved upon the model and motivated me to write a second edition with more stories, more tips and the experiences of more solo travelers.

You will find other voices in this book. You will hear from solo travelers who are younger and older than me. You will hear from men as well as women. And you will learn what I have learned over the last year.

I hope you enjoy what I consider to be the "new and improved" *Solo Traveler's Handbook*.

Hatching out of one of Salvador Dalí's eggs at the House Museum Salvador Dalí in Cadaqués, Costa Brava, Spain.

The Backstory

It was February of 2009 and I was sitting on the couch licking my wounds.

My husband, Ron, had passed away in December 2006 and on that cold Saturday afternoon, over two years later, I felt myself falling into another cycle of grief. But this time, I'd had enough. I got angry. When would it end? And then, for whatever reason, I thought "well, I guess I'm traveling solo."

Ron and I had traveled extensively with our children. We traveled as we could afford — which was not fancy. Early travels included road trips and camping across Canada. We went east to Newfoundland and west to British Columbia. When money became a little more available, we immediately spent it on a six-week camping trip through Europe. We knew how to stretch a travel dollar. In 2001/02, after selling our small business, we rented a Volkswagen Pop-up Camper, homeschooled our youngest and traveled Europe for 10 months. Our other sons joined us at various points along the way. We were "The Drifters" with kids.

But in 2009, I no longer had Ron as my travel mate and the kids were grown. With a wanderlust that went back to my pre-teens, I decided, that February afternoon, that I would travel again as I had in my twenties. I would travel solo.

As a writer with a basic knowledge of the online world, I guess the next step was to be expected. I picked up the computer lying beside me and Googled "solo travel". I found no one writing from personal experience. I decided at that moment to start my blog, *Solo Traveler*.

The entire Solo Traveler Project — this book, the blog, the Solo Travel Society on Facebook and speaking engagements — is a personal journey as well as a call to action. I urge you to break the bounds of convention and expectations; to claim the right to be alone, whether for a day or a lifetime; and to travel solo.

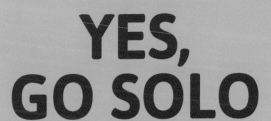

YES,
GO SOLO

While at any given time there are thousands of adventurous travelers discovering the world solo, there are also tens of thousands wondering whether they can. With few exceptions, the answer is yes.

The contrasts of Havana.

My Lesson in Havana

I stepped off the plane in Havana at 11:30 p.m., passed through Immigration and took a taxi into the city. It dropped me in Old Havana, where the street turns into a pedestrian mall. The driver pointed and claimed my hotel was there but, as I looked around, I couldn't see it. The street was deserted. Just me and my carry-on in the dark. Taking a few steps, I heard the sound of my suitcase wheels rolling on the cobblestones echoing off the buildings. I stopped. This didn't feel safe.

But it was no safer standing still, so I moved on. Nothing was lit. I walked right past my hotel until I found a security guard who directed me to backtrack. Walking in the opposite direction I found my hotel and made a mental note: never arrive in a new city after dark.

This was my first solo trip since my twenties. At 49, I didn't think twice about traveling alone. However, my first 24 hours in Havana made me think I should have.

Having found my hotel, I checked in and made it to my room. A room without windows. I sat on the bed and looked at the four walls. The room was clean. The furniture was fine. The bathroom was very nice. It was all newly renovated as the travel agent had told me but...no windows? It had not occurred to me to make such a request. I also hadn't thought about arriving in the dark to a deserted pedestrian mall. What else had I not prepared for?

The following morning I asked to be moved to a room with a window, went to a bank and struggled through a currency exchange, ate a terrible meal and got lost in a street pattern that made no sense to me; it was all too much. I returned to my hotel, called my travel agent and requested to be moved to an all-inclusive resort.

By late afternoon the next day I realized that the agent would not be returning my call. I had been politely dismissed. Fortunately, by that time, I was glad. I was enamored with Havana, an old, derelict city that was being lovingly restored.

You see, after I made the call requesting the move, I didn't just sit in my hotel room waiting for a reply. I went for another walk through Old Havana, this time with direction. I headed toward the Capitol Building and enjoyed watching boys playing baseball on the Capitol grounds. They couldn't do that in Washington or Ottawa. That was the turning point for me. From there I headed to the waterfront and walked along the Malecón. Then I wandered back through Old Havana, exploring. Suddenly, getting lost was a good thing. That evening I ate dinner at my hotel. The food fell somewhere between international cuisine and Cuban. It suited me and helped me relax.

In the end, I was taken by the Cuban culture, so different from home and yet in the same time zone and only three and a half hours away. I was charmed by people who clearly struggled with their country and, at the same time, celebrated it.

My arrival in Havana and moment of panic was simply that, a moment, one I often feel when I arrive in a new city. But, like it did in Havana, the panic always subsides. I learned the lesson of patience on that trip: a lesson that serves me well because it is with patience that the most wonderful adventures begin.

Who is Solo Travel For?

You.

Extroverts:
enjoy time for reflection or take on the world.

Introverts:
gain social confidence or find time to be truly alone.

Singles:
use the freedom you're fortunate to have and meet new people.

Couples:
go individually, grow and invigorate your relationship.

20-somethings:
discover independence.

30-somethings:
figure life out.

Mid-lifers:
rediscover yourself after decades of responsibility.

Seniors:
live a sensational third act.

Everyone:
fulfill your travel dreams.

Why Go Solo?

The Practical Perks

While you may discover solo travel by chance — because you don't have anyone to travel with when you have the time and the money — you will likely do so again by choice. After all, solo travel is all about you.

- You do what you want, when you want. You're on your own schedule.

- You're free to meet locals and other travelers — and, because you're alone, it happens often and easily. We'll get into how and why later in the book.

- You're able to focus on the destination and all it offers without distractions.

- You enjoy periods of quiet for reading, art, reflection... you have as much downtime as you want.

- You follow your own interests, be they bungee jumping or combing archives.

- You receive special treatment as locals often go out of their way to enhance your solo travel experience.

Okay, maybe some of the above can apply to those traveling with a companion as well, but when you travel solo they definitely apply. On a practical level, solo travel frees you to travel your way. It's not about being selfish. Solo travel offers so much more. Read on.

The Personal Discoveries

Solo travel lets you explore who you are when no one is looking. At home, family, friends, employers and colleagues influence your actions. Traveling alone, you escape the influence of others and live free to make your own choices.

As you make your choices you learn about yourself: how you like to spend your time, how you feel about things, your personal rhythm. You get to know yourself better and discover new passions as well as strengths you didn't know you had. Along the way you may collect a few souvenirs like new skills and self-confidence.

The Public Challenge
Solo travel challenges the "single" stigma.

We are a population that is increasingly single. People are getting married later. We are marrying multiple times with periods of singlehood in between. Some choose to be single for life and others find themselves single by loss. With so many singles living great lives, why should there be a stigma attached to being so?

Solo travelers defy that stigma one trip at a time. By traveling alone you help redefine the image of the single experience.

At the amazing Taj Mahal in India.

It's About the Freedom
by Allen Bullard
30-something, Ireland

For me it's about total freedom: being able to go where I want, when I want, with no set itinerary. I like to travel with no fixed plan and solo travel allows me to do this.

My last trip was to Africa. It's a part of the world I had wanted to see for a while, but it is such a large and diverse continent that I had no idea where to start. A random conversation ended with me deciding to walk the Camino de Santiago. So I spent September walking 800 km across Spain. From there I took a ferry to Morocco where I spent a few weeks before crossing the Sahara and on to Mauritania. The next few months included Senegal, Guinea Bissau, Mali, Burkina Faso and Benin.

Leaving Spain, my only definite plan was to spend some time in Mali. Everywhere else was based on stories or recommendations from other travelers I met along the way.

This is not always the easiest part of the world to travel through and it obviously gets a fraction of the tourists that you'll see elsewhere. Despite (or maybe because of) this, I had an amazing time. Stepping outside of my comfort zone forced me to be more independent and to take responsibility for organizing things myself. Being in places that have few or no tourists pushed me into much closer interaction with the local people and culture.

My experience of West Africa was one of smiling, friendly and helpful people everywhere I went, even though I spoke virtually no French. It was also one of the most educational travel experiences I've ever had: the Africa we see portrayed in the Western media is a long way from the reality I observed.

I had some amazing experiences. From getting stranded on a random island in Guinea for 12 hours after our boat got lost, to partying until 9:00 a.m. in Bamako with newfound friends, to attending a local Friday night voodoo festival in Benin. As is always the case when I travel, it was the people I met along the way who really made the trip.

My experience of solo travel is that even though you start alone you're never that way for long. On the contrary, every trip I've taken has given me a new bunch of lifelong friends.

Allen in Dogon country in Mali, one of his favourite places in west Africa.

Dream Trips to Real Trips in 7 Steps

If travel is your dream it's important to go.

Don't put things off. You don't know the future so live the present well (with a healthy financial respect for the future, of course). Here are 7 steps for great short- or long-term trips.

Dream. Dream wildly. The bigger the dream, the better the trip.

Talk. Tell people about your dreams, what you want to do and why. The more you explain it to others the more real it will become and the better you'll understand why you must go.

Schedule. Carve out the time you need. You may only need your regular vacation days or you may need a leave of absence. Be creative and you can negotiate what you require in life. (Oh, did I say life? Of course, I meant travel!)

Save. Saving for travel is penny-pinching with a huge prize. Read about saving money in the next section.

Research. Expand your dream by watching films, reading books and blogs about your destination and participating in online forums. You'll discover, through others, just how fantastic your trip can be and you'll learn the practical steps required to make it happen.

Plan. Bare-bones logistics is all you really need (though I respect those who pull together more). You need to know how you'll get there, where you will stay the first night and how you'll manage your insurance, documents and money. Beyond that, planning is all about your comfort level.

Go. Always have your passport ready. Buy your plane/train/bus tickets. Book your accommodation. Go.

Travel is really not that difficult. Go and enjoy! Don't miss the moment.

PLANNING MAKES A DIFFERENCE

Psyched to travel solo? Then get ready to go.

No Time Zone. No Jet Lag. Living the FIB Time Warp.

Can we turn back time? Can we live as twentysomethings in our fifties? Can we travel across six time zones without jet lag?

Before my 2010 trip to Valencia, Spain for the Benicàssim Music Festival my answer would have been "no." Afterwards? Well, let's just say I gained a new sense of the possible.

The FIB, Festival Internacional de Benicàssim, is four days of pop, rock and rap. A huge draw for the Brits as well as the Spanish, this festival taught me that time can lose all meaning. Stimulated by the music as well as the scene, I never felt jet-lagged. I survived on very few hours of sleep each night. To bed by 3:00 a.m. (or 4:00) and, of course, up early to take in local attractions.

At The FIB, kids screamed. Music pulsed. At times my clothes literally shook from the bass notes. From 6:00 p.m. to 6:00 a.m., The FIB offered up some of the hottest bands in Europe in a four-day party. This was a press trip and there were other travel and music bloggers there as well. With press passes in hand, we went to the pit in front of the stage to take pictures of the various bands, including Vampire Weekend, The Specials, The Prodigy, Dizzee Rascal, and Gorillaz.

But, of course, I also took off solo to explore The FIB my way.

Wandering to the far stage (there were three), I stood at the back of the crowd to listen. I had no idea who the band was but they were singing in English and they were great! I made my way forward. Then to the very front. I listened to their whole performance. It wasn't long before I was desperate to know who they were but, being considerate of the crowd that was totally with the band, I held back until the end. Then, I turned around and started asking people:

Inglés? Habla inglés?

I found a small group of four who did speak English and told me the story. I was listening to The Sunday Drivers. But this wasn't just any performance of The Sunday Drivers – a wildly popular Spanish band. It was their farewell show. This is why they were the only band I saw that performed encores. And, at the end, family and friends poured onto the stage for hugs in celebration. It was a scene.

I had an absolutely fantastic time in Benicàssim. What I learned there was that time is indeed relative: relative to what you are doing. If you're having a great time, the hour, time zones, jet lag – they all mean nothing.

Dancing at the FIB – Benicassim, Spain.

Tips: Take 'em or Toss 'em

As I write this book, I am trying to cover all possible scenarios for all potential travel abilities, anxiety levels and destinations. Therefore, the information is detailed and yet, it may not be detailed enough. It's an impossible task.

Some tips will apply in some situations but not in others. Some may not be useful on your next trip but could be very valuable on a future trip. I encourage you to use as many tips as seem right for you and not to worry about leaving the rest behind.

Travel within your own comfort level. Always use your best judgment.

Make Solo Your MO

Let's put it on the table: people have concerns about traveling solo. I'll admit it: I have concerns at times as well. But I plan and I give myself time at every new destination to settle in and feel comfortable. And then, the most wonderful travel experiences ensue.

People tell me that:

- Traveling alone doesn't feel safe.
- Dining alone is awkward.
- Traveling alone is lonely.
- Traveling solo I have to be responsible for everything.
- If I go alone:
  - There's no one to share experiences with.
  - There's no one to share memories with.

I understand. I've experienced each of these concerns from time to time. But, in my mind, the pros far outweigh the cons. Thanks to a few tactics I've discovered in my travels, and the people I've met along the way, none of these concerns have warranted any real hesitation about solo travel.

So let's get started. Let's explore how to make solo your MO (your modus operandi).

---

66 *I travel solo to become a 'better me'. I find that I am more open to new cultures and people when I travel. I go out there with an open mind: I am a clean slate. I have discovered what makes me tick, what my priorities are, what matters most in my life. I have met such wonderful people and even when experiences haven't been all good, they have been important and necessary in my life. I wouldn't trade solo travel for anything. I come home from a journey and immediately look forward to the next trip! Travel is like breathing to me: it's an absolute must!* **99**

Stephanie Phillips
40-something, California, USA

When to Go

Traveling in the high season is better than not traveling at all but not as good as traveling when the crowds are gone. Traveling in the low season, the weather is probably poor – either too hot or too cold — but there are no crowds to fight. Traveling in the shoulder season, between high and low seasons is, in my mind, the sweet spot for solo travel.

The shoulder season makes almost everything easier. Almost. There will be some museums or sights that are closed until high season. You'll miss the occasional "classic highlight" but you'll get much as compensation. You'll get to relax as you travel. And you won't need to get up early to beat the crowds.

To find out when the shoulder season is and when you enter the low season, check the hours of operation of a specific sight or rates for hotels. When opening hours shorten, you're in the shoulder season. When hotel rates go up, you're in the high season.

It was very early spring when I circumnavigated Lake Ontario.
The shoulder season: good weather, few crowds, a fabulous time to go.

Ditching the Digital World to Ramble in the Rain

I'm online almost all the time.

My writing practice, my blog and social media – they are all demanding and I sometimes wonder what I'm missing by not giving my mind enough wander time. This is why I implemented my annual Digital Detox a few years ago. Every autumn I go offline completely for as many days as I can afford. In 2009 I spent four days offline in the Lake District of England.

The Lake District has a romantic past. William Wordsworth and the Lake Poets drew attention to this special area in the Northwest corner of England during the 19th century. It has since become a destination for nature lovers and walking enthusiasts everywhere. With no history as a hiker, off I went.

I discovered that there is something strangely addictive about walking the hills, or fells, as they are called locally. On my first day I spent almost four hours covering a mere 10k. After a couple of hours walking it appeared that I had reached the top so I took photos of my success. As I continued along the path to descend, I discovered that I had to go up some more. I did half of the walk in the rain and all of it walking through water. Drenched and a bit frustrated, I wondered: "is this fun? Do I like this? Is the notion of walking better than the actual doing?" Yet, I awoke the next day eager to go out again.

As the saying goes, "there is no bad weather, only bad clothing." So, taking full responsibility for my wet feet from day one, I bought a pair of waterproof hiking boots the next morning and set out again. It was a wise investment. It rained numerous times every day I was there and the paths I walked were often streams, which makes sense given all the lakes.

My destination on day two was Grasmere. My route was the Coffin Walk, the path along which people from Ambleside carried their dead to a consecrated burial ground in the nineteenth century. By the time I reached the lovely Rydal Tearoom, not a quarter of the way to Grasmere, I was drenched again: except for my feet, of course.

I hung my jacket near the high-efficiency fireplace, ordered a pot of tea and sat down on a comfortable couch. Soon two men sat on the couch opposite and, as is usual for me, I started a conversation. It wasn't long before we set off together toward Grasmere. Chris and Peter of Liverpool were wonderful company. They gave me a history of the fells and pointed out details of the flora and architecture in the small cottages we passed that I would never have noticed had I made the trip alone.

I hiked one more day up the pike of Wansfell. Unfortunately, it was in a cloud when I got there. But, later in the day, on my descent, I had a wonderful view of Lake Windermere. When I saw the panorama that I had thought would elude me that day, the views I had enjoyed, the pleasure of physical exertion and the satisfaction of having walked for three days straight, all converged and I was in love. The Lake District now holds a truly special place in my heart.

As for my Digital Detox, there were no shakes, no anxious moments. Walking requires focus. It demanded my attention to get my footing right, to follow the map and instructions, to stay on course and to take in the beauty. It was easy to leave thoughts of work behind. Ditching the digital world can be achieved, especially when walking the fells.

It tends to rain a lot in the off/shoulder season of The Lake District in the United Kingdom, but I still had a wonderful time.

Where to Go

What are the best destinations for solo travelers? I am asked this question all the time. And, of course, there is no one right answer to this question. It depends on the individual's interests, physical abilities, financial resources, time available and travel experience.

Here's how I break it down for people.

First time solo travelers with no travel experience
If you're not only a first time solo traveler but also quite new to travel, I suggest that you stay close to home. Start by taking baby steps to build your confidence. Try a weekend getaway. Drive or take a bus or train to another town, city, province or state and explore. You will be doing so in a similar language and culture which minimizes the challenges of solo travel.

As you travel, practice some of these basic solo travel techniques:
- Stay at a hostel or B&B and have breakfast with strangers.
- Join groups for short periods of time. Take a museum tour or a cooking class. Anything of that nature will deliver a really social experience.
- Research coffee shops and restaurants with communal tables, so you can meet people in a casual setting.
- If you're feeling really adventurous, go out and see some live music in the evening.
- Don't forget to give yourself some quiet time as well and take note of how it feels to be independent, strong and capable.
- Please refer to the safety section of this book, do a bit of research and head out.

First time solo travelers with travel experience OR experienced solo travelers with no experience abroad
These two categories of solo travelers have the same best destination in my mind so I've joined them together.

If you've never traveled solo but are already a traveler, you need to develop your solo travel skills. You know what travel is, how airports work, that tourism bureaus are typically near train stations and much more. A lot of your travel knowledge has become instinctive. Your challenge will be being alone.

If you've traveled solo but only close to home, your learning curve is on the other side of the coin. Your challenge will be to negotiate transportation and foreign currency but you will feel pretty comfortable with being alone.

In both cases, I suggest a destination with a familiar culture and language. For North Americans, the United Kingdom, Ireland and many places in Europe, such as Amsterdam, are great options. However, as Jodi describes on page 26, Southeast Asia has become a popular option for many.

Seasoned solo travelers wanting to broaden their experience
Once you've traveled solo both at home and abroad, you're really ready to widen your horizons and explore more challenging destinations. But where? Check your bucket list and choose your destination based on the money and time you have available. If you choose a really adventurous destination, it may be worth taking a tour at the beginning of your trip, learning how your destination works and then venturing out on your own.

Follow your passion
Whatever level of experience you have, solo travel is often better when serving your passion. Whether it's food or nature or volunteer work, include your passion in your travels to make them all the more special.

Hiking and the outdoors has become a new passion of mine – Patagonia, Chile.

   " *Mainland Southeast Asia, which comprises Thailand, Laos, Cambodia, Myanmar, Malaysia and other countries, is the first destination I recommend to solo travelers looking to venture outside North America. Not only does the landscape impress, but the culture is fascinating and encourages much learning of new customs. The food is cheap and street food is a huge part of daily culture, meaning that it is accessible and safe. There is a very developed tourist infrastructure already in place, making travel within the region very easy. From budget airlines to endless bus, boat or shared ride options, it's one of the most friendly and navigable regions to roam through.*

More importantly, I feel safe there as a solo female traveler. I use common sense of course, as I would in North America, but I have found locals very helpful and walking around alone in cities comfortable. I have spent almost 2.5 years in Southeast Asia, and my travel options remain infinite and my smile wide. **"**

Jodi Ettenberg
30-something world traveler
LegalNomads.com

Money: Meaning and Managing

Money, that piece of paper or plastic in your pocket, has no value until you buy something with it. Then, its value is up to you. Is it:

- One taxi ride or public transit and a latte?
- One week at a resort in high season or a two-week road trip?
- A DSLR camera or a quality point & shoot and good walking shoes?

As a solo traveler, you, based on your values alone, choose how to budget your trip. There is no need to compromise with someone else. You set the budget and you decide when to break it. And break it you will.

The key to breaking the budget successfully is in knowing how to make trades. You can come in under budget in one place to break it in another. It's usually quite easy.

Money and Stress

The way we think about and use money can cause stress or relieve it. Spending more than you can afford on a trip will cause stress as you pay for it when you return. Spending a lot on travel gear, even if you can afford it, can cause stress if you worry about losing the gear while you're traveling. However, spending more money than normal on accommodation in a city where you have safety concerns will reduce stress. Splurging on a taxi late at night also strikes the right stress/safety vs. money balance. Spend your money with these considerations in mind.

Money and Points

With all the rewards programs available, it is possible to travel a lot while spending only a little. People who do this really well are called Travel Hackers. Look at the resources at the end of the book for links on travel hacking.

Saving Money for Travel

Some people dream about travel and others do it. It's not that the doers are independently wealthy, but they know how to save. Here are some tips to get you the needed travel dollars:

- Define your dream destination. Put a photo of it on your fridge or your screen saver. Keep it top of mind and then weigh every purchase against that dream.
- Set up an automatic withdrawal from your regular bank account and send the money to a dedicated travel account. Would you miss twenty dollars a week? That adds up to $1,040 a year: enough for a single person to do something fun for a week or maybe more depending on your taste.
- Don't think you can afford twenty dollars a week? Make and bring your lunch, go back to regular coffee rather than lattes, walk or cycle rather than drive or take transit. Each of these changes is a healthy lifestyle choice and will easily save you more than twenty dollars a week.
- Buy with a credit card that has no annual fee and offers cash back on purchases. Pay the card off in full every month and don't shop at more expensive stores just to get the reimbursement. Add your cash back to your travel fund.
- Use the library to cut your entertainment costs by borrowing books and DVDs.
- Hold potluck dinners rather than providing everything when you entertain.
- Drop your long distance package from your phone bill and use Skype. It may even make sense to eliminate your home phone completely.
- Dine out at lunch rather than dinner, especially at fine restaurants. The quality is the same but the cost is often much lower.
- Know how you react in an impulse buy situation. Some people are stopped by seeing cash leave their hands, others by the prospect of using a credit card. Carry whichever form of money you are less likely to use.
- In the same vein, have a "spend no change" policy. It will add up nicely in a jar. This is especially true in Canada and the UK where there are dollar and pound coins.
- Sell your unneeded stuff online. It's amazing what you can sell and it will be cash right into your pocket. Sell many things at once to be efficient with your time.
- Write down everything you spend. Just knowing how much you're spending and where, will help you save.
- Take on a second job or volunteer for overtime, then put all extra earnings in your travel fund; this is particularly useful when saving for long-term trips since you get a long break after working so intensely.

I'm sure that you can come up with your own unique ways to save travel money.

Setting a Budget

Whether you're financially established or a struggling student, at some point you need to decide what your trip will cost and if you can afford it. This is where reality challenges your dreams and your bank account is the judge.

The easiest way to budget your trip is to look at the cost of getting to your destination first and then add your daily expenses. Determining your daily expenses may be difficult to do online. This is where travel guides such as Lonely Planet and Frommer's excel. As a person with far too many travel guides that are out-of-date, I suggest you borrow one from the library.

In your daily expenses you need to consider:

Accommodation: Whether you'll stay at hostels or expensive hotels, these costs are relatively easy to determine.

Food: You don't want to live on porridge for days at a time (I met one traveler who did) but you don't need fine restaurants every day either. Determine what you want to spend daily, knowing that you will spend more on some days and less on others. Find out if breakfast is included in the cost of your accommodation.

Transportation: Local transportation varies greatly. Cabs make sense in some cities but may be an unnecessary expense in others.

Sightseeing: From wine tours to museum visits to city tours, you need to anticipate approximately how much you will spend. Research the costs of big-ticket items in particular so that they don't come as a shock.

Entertainment: You know yourself and your style of travel best. If you plan on clubbing, dancing, fine dining or drinking, then factor in the cost of club entrance fees, drinks, tips, etc.

Multiply your average daily expenses by the number of days you'll be at your destination, add your cost of getting there, any visa fees to enter the country, and recommended vaccinations and you'll have an approximate budget. Also factor in any gear you need to buy specifically for your trip: hiking gear, extreme weather clothes, raincoats, etc.

Drawing up a budget doesn't have much value unless you stick to it, so track your expenses daily. This can be done on your laptop, on your smartphone or in your journal. What matters is that you know where you stand regarding your budget. It can make the difference between returning with regrets or with a fabulous souvenir you didn't realize you could afford.

Managing Money

Carrying cash and paying for things is an issue for solo travelers. You alone are responsible for doing both safely. You have a number of options:

- Debit cards which access your bank account directly.
- Credit cards which you must pay when you return.
- Prepaid credit cards or products like a Thomas Cook Cash Passport. You load the card with the amount of money you want to have available.
- Cash. It's good to be able to pay in the local currency as you will get better prices. Carrying some US dollars is good for emergencies.

Most of these options include transaction fees of various sorts. Check with your financial institution to understand them. If you travel often or are going to developing countries, it will be worth researching which banks have lower or no fees. When possible, use local ATMs rather than currency exchange counters in airports and train terminals, as these tend to be more expensive. To minimize complications when you travel:

- Have more than one means of getting cash, such as a debit card and credit card or two debit cards that use different international systems.
- Have more than one credit card with you. It's a good idea to have a Visa card and a MasterCard since they are both widely accepted.
- Call your credit card companies before you go to let them know where you're traveling and for how long.
- Know the exchange rate before you land so you can withdraw the appropriate amount of cash.

- Keep the telephone numbers of your credit card companies and banks with your travel paperwork so that you can call them immediately if you lose your cards. Scan and e-mail these to yourself so you can easily access them.
- Consider how you will top up a prepaid credit card or move cash around when traveling. For security reasons, using public Wi-Fi is not advisable for this purpose. If you are visiting friends along the way, plan to use their secure Internet. In a pinch, I have requested and been granted access to the Internet at a bank.
- Consider the cost of each system when deciding which you will use. If you travel a lot you may want to have a premium account that allows international withdrawals for a flat fee.
- Don't carry more money with you than you think necessary when you're out for the day. Keep it in two separate locations, for example, a pocket and a purse. Men, don't keep your wallet in your back pocket.
- Carry a small secondary wallet (a mugger's wallet) so that you have hidden cash at all times.
- Keep some of your financial resources in your money belt or room safe.

One has to spend money wisely but, once in a while, it's worth treating yourself to accommoidation like the Hotel Castell d'Emporda in Costa Brava, Spain.

Where to Lay your Head

For the typical traveler, accommodation is a matter of taste and budget. For the solo traveler, it is much more. Your choice of accommodation will affect your travel experience greatly. Here are the options and what you can expect.

B&Bs

Bed & Breakfasts (or guesthouses as they are sometimes called) are often located in private homes and are typically more expensive than hostels but less expensive than hotels. A bedroom, a shared or private bathroom and breakfast are offered. There is usually a sitting room to be shared by the guests and a communal table for breakfast, making this style of accommodation ideal for solo travelers. You are on your own for all other meals of the day.

B&B owners are usually very friendly and a great source of information on their town or city. Many B&B owners belong to an association. There are a number of rating services online but no standard that is widely used around the world. Luxury B&Bs certainly exist, but so do very undesirable ones. Check the reviews and choose carefully.

Hostels

Hostels are great for those on a budget and interested in meeting people. Once for the young only, they now welcome people of all ages. I regularly meet people in their 40s, 50s and even 60s at hostels.

Hostels run the gamut from quirky and stylish to very, very basic. Some only offer dormitories and bunk beds at a low cost but others also have private and semi-private rooms. Breakfast and free Wi-Fi are often included in the price, as is access to a kitchen so you can cook for yourself.

With common lounges, hostels are great places to meet people and exchange information. Travelers learn from each other, sharing tips and advice on their favorite places, what they thought was worth the time or money and what wasn't.

Hotels

You don't have to look far to realize that hotels range greatly in quality. The hotel star system is intended to give you a sense of the quality of a hotel: the more stars, the better the hotel in terms of the amenities it offers.

Unfortunately, the star system varies greatly and there is no standardized international system. The number of stars a hotel has is often determined by the local tourist board or automobile association making star ratings more relevant within a region than between regions or countries. As a result, a five-star hotel in some countries may compare to your understanding of a three-star. The star system may also focus on amenities, not charm. A wonderful hotel without a pool may not rate well but could be the exact place you want to stay. Unless you're dealing with a major chain or are comparing one resort to another in the same area, the star system may have limited value.

Hotels tend to be less social than other options but they usually have trustworthy people with local knowledge to answer your questions.

Apartment Rentals

Renting an apartment is a great way to connect with a community while traveling. Rentals start at a few days but can run for a number of months. Their cost varies widely based on size and location. They are usually well equipped so that you will have just about everything you have at home.

The downside of rentals is that they don't have a social aspect built in as hostels and B&Bs do, nor do they have someone at the front desk to answer questions like hotels do. On the other hand, you can go to the same bakery, fruit and vegetable shop and cafe daily and become known in the community; the people you meet at these places become your go-to resources. Full payment for rentals may be required in advance either by credit card or cash. A deposit may also be required.

Couchsurfing

Couchsurfing gives you a local experience. As with a B&B, you stay in someone's home. You may get a bed or a couch but, in this case, they won't charge you.

Register on a site like CouchSurfing.org to get connected to other couchsurfers and hosts. Add as much detail as possible to your profile and participate in the community online and off; there are CouchSurfing events in some cities.

Be cautious with couchsurfing. Look at a prospective host's references to see whether they've been vouched for. Look to their response rate as an indicator of how trustworthy they are. Check the "couch" information field to confirm what kind of accommodation you'll get. Message a person you'd like to surf with and carry on a conversation to get a feel for who they are. Ask them about smoking, household pets or other potential allergens. Consider meeting your prospective host for a coffee before staying at their place.

Being a member of CouchSurfing.org, opens you up to an interesting community of travelers. Even if you stay at a hostel or hotel, you can use this community to contact a local and get together with them for a coffee or meal to learn about their hometown.

---

66 *WWOOFing (World Wide Opportunities on Organic Farms) is truly a great option for solo travelers. Living with a host family provides you with genuine immersion into local life, bringing you companionship and helping to avoid the loneliness that some people feel when traveling alone for long periods. Outside working hours, you are free to do as you please, allowing lots of opportunities for exploring and "me time" as well.* 99

Sean
20-something, London, United Kingdom
Gozimba.com

Others

There are many other options when it comes to accommodation. Though I have not used these personally, I have heard great reports from people who have house-swapped, stayed in monasteries and in university dormitories.

HUNTINGTON **CITY TOWNSHIP**
PUBLIC LIBRARY
255 WEST PARK DRIVE
HUNTINGTON, IN 46750

Hostels typically have common rooms (foreground), shared dining and free use of computers with Internet access.

Yoga. Cow. Ohm.

It was 7:45 a.m. and our 1¾ hour yoga practice was coming to a close. Having been silent since nine o'clock the night before, we prepared for our first public sound in almost eleven hours. Led by Yogi Vishvketu, we breathed in deeply and exhaled a beautiful ohm. We did it a second time. In, out. And then, with our third slow inhale complete, just as we were ready for our final ohm, a cow outside expressed it for us. Yes, the moo of a cow actually sounds surprisingly like ohm. The entire class broke into laughter.

This little story sums up my experience at Anand Prakash Yoga Ashram in Rishikesh, India. There was the physical challenge of three and a half hours of yoga each day, spiritual relaxation through silence and meditation and laughter. Beyond the laughter yoga that was part of many classes, there was the laughter of friends sharing meals at the Ashram, chai masala in tea rooms, and excursions in the town and the Himalayan foothills.

The Ashram Routine

The day starts early at the Ashram. Rising at 5:15 a.m., I would make my way to the yoga studio by 5:45, allowing enough time to relax and meditate before class began at six o'clock. The class runs until 7:45 a.m., which allows 15 minutes to get your dishes from your room and get to the dining hall for breakfast. After breakfast, there is a fire puja (a ritual) for about a half hour. Then, free time until lunch and free time in the afternoon until four o'clock when there is another 1¾ hour yoga class. Dinner is at six o'clock and a Kiirtan (chanting) is practiced on some evenings at seven. By nine o'clock silence is observed again until the next morning after breakfast.

Yes, the early morning is completely silent. As the students move to the yoga class, get their dishes and have breakfast, no words are exchanged. Smiles, yes. But no words. It's surprisingly pleasant.

Time between classes is used for journaling, meditating and reading. Ashram life involves solitary pursuits within a communal context.

Adjusting to Ashram Life

I slipped into the pattern of Ashram life very easily. This was a surprise to me. I had never done anything like it. I have been self-employed forever, with no one telling me what to do and when. I wondered if I could adjust to a pre-set schedule. But I did. And I welcomed the routine. I welcomed the early mornings (me?), the silence, the simple but satisfying food and three and a half hours of yoga a day. The only real challenge was sitting cross-legged for meals. I had hoped, by the end of my stay, to make it through a complete meal without stretching my legs in front of me, but it just didn't happen.

Enjoying Rishikesh and Surrounding Area

I probably didn't do as much reading, meditating and journaling at the Ashram as I should have because I was so taken with the surrounding area, the foothills of the Himalayas. Tears welled up in my eyes when I first saw them from the rooftop patio of Anand Prakash. I was in the Himalayas. I couldn't believe it!

If I'd had a second week at the Ashram, I'm sure I would have settled down to the more contemplative activities but there was the market to explore, hiking nearby, many wonderful gardens where I enjoyed chai masala and Rajiji National Park where I went on safari and saw an elephant in the wild. The Ashram, Rishikesh, the mountains, the routine – I was taken with it all!

Cows and characters in Rishikesh, India.

Packing: You Are Your Own Sherpa

I know. A carry-on? Much too small, right? Some people can't do it, but in my opinion, it's a must. I can't emphasize enough just how beneficial it is to pack lightly. Whether you use a suitcase or a backpack, conforming to carry-on standards has many advantages:

- Quick electronic check-in.
- No wait at the luggage carousel.
- Easy transfers between planes and terminals.
- The possibility of taking local transit to airports.
- No need for help at your hotel, hostel, or B&B.
- Your luggage won't be lost by the airlines.
- No extra luggage fees from the airlines.

And

- You won't fumble with luggage, which makes you a more capable traveler.

But

- Be careful and considerate. Airlines are becoming stricter about their carry-on rules. Follow the weight rules, don't overstuff your items and leave space for others. One item in the overhead and one at your feet is reasonable.

Carry-On or Backpack?

If you are city traveling, a carry-on suitcase is easy to roll along the streets. Adventure travel or travel that involves many cities and transfers may be easier with a backpack. Bottom line, it's what you're comfortable with.

Neither has to be particularly expensive. I spent forty dollars on my carry-on six years ago and it's taken over twenty trips with me. My 40-liter backpack is newer and a little more technical. I spent $130 on it and I love it.

I also use a daypack for carrying essentials on a flight and for use on a daily basis.

Sample Packing List

You don't need to pack much more for a month than you do for a week, if you are strategic.

Packing List Essentials

- All paperwork: hotel confirmations, flight information, passport and travel insurance details.
- Global plug adapter.
- eReader: Kindle, Kobo, iPad.
- Journal and pen.
- Computer and AC adapter (optional).
- Phone unlocked for worldwide use and charger (recommended).
- Camera and batteries or charger.
- Prescription medication, vitamins, supplements, water bottle.
- Tiny first aid kit.
- Shampoo, conditioner, hair product, face cream, makeup, deodorant, toothbrush, toothpaste, floss, brush, razor, shave soap.
- Safety whistle and doorstop.

Packing List for Women

To be pack-worthy, everything you take must work well with other things. To have clothes for a range of activities that work together, choose one color palette. Working with a base color like black or brown along with a contrasting color, such as grey or beige, and an accent color, ensures that everything you're carrying works together.

- Shoes: two pairs total. One pair of street shoes (or sandals) and one pair of dressier shoes. (If you need hiking boots, wear them on the plane. You can tie them onto your carry-on or backpack and wear your street shoes at your destination.) Shoes make or break an outfit and shoe comfort makes or breaks a trip; choose them carefully. Many bars, clubs and upscale restaurants all over the world have a "no flip-flop" policy, so pack accordingly.

- Pants: three pairs total or two pairs and one dress or skirt. (Wear your most comfortable on the plane.)
- Tops: five tops, one light sweater and one camisole (that works as an under layer for warmth and under a jacket for a dressier look).
- One cardigan OR light jacket that can dress up or down depending on jeans/pants and accessories.
- Belt, inexpensive jewelry, scarf or scarves to dress up casual clothes.
- Pashmina scarf. It has so many uses from head cover to beach cover-up to protection from a wind storm.
- Umbrella, scarf, gloves, rain pants, hat, vest and sunglasses (depending on weather at your destinations).
- Bathing suit.
- Pajamas, underwear, socks.
- Sanitary products.

It sounds like a lot but it's not. When you return, determine what you didn't use and don't pack it again.

Packing List for Men
A man's packing list is not a lot different from a woman's except that it's easier. There is not as much nuance in what a man wears: throw a blazer onto a guy wearing jeans and a t-shirt, and he looks great. So, here's the men's packing list.

- Shoes: two pairs total. One pair of street shoes (or sandals) and one pair of dressier shoes. (As above, if you need hiking boots, wear them on the plane.) Only bring shoes that have proven themselves comfortable.
- Pants/shorts: three pairs total. You know your style but one pair should not be jeans.
- 4 t-shirts. (Make sure at least one of them is white to wear under a dress shirt). If you're going someplace tropical or humid, make sure that they are very light and pack more of them.
- 1 golf shirt or casual shirt with a collar.

- 1 dress shirt.
- One blazer. (This is optional, of course, but really useful. Choose a light fabric.)
- Belt and tie (if you're into that look).
- Umbrella, scarf, gloves, rain pants, hat, vest and sunglasses (depending on the weather at your destinations).
- Bathing suit.
- Underwear, pajamas and socks.

For Longer-Term or Hostel Travel
- Silk sheet to sleep in.
- Padlock for your things.
- High absorbency towel.
- Headlamp or flashlight.
- A few feet of duct tape can come in quite handy.
- A couple of resealable plastic bags.

Packing Light Tips
- Don't pack the bulky things: wear them on the plane.
- Follow carry-on luggage rules according to your airline. This is getting more and more difficult. Some airlines have reduced the allowance to 8 kilograms so you may have to check your bags regardless.
- Watch the restrictions on the size of bottled liquids and other items you want to carry on board.
- Pack less and rinse clothes out when necessary.
- Replenish toiletries, even clothes, on the road.

More on my Pashmina Scarf

My white cotton pashmina-style scarf gets special mention. Unless it's winter, it goes everywhere with me and has functioned as a:

- Head cover in religious sites.
- Face protector from wind and sand in the desert.
- Towel.
- Pillow protector in a dodgy hostel.
- Cover-up on the beach.
- Accessory to dress up a t-shirt.
- Scarf for warmth.

The scarf protected me from wind and sand in Wadi Rum – Jordan.

Don't ruin your fun by...

Opting for fashion over function. If you fuss too much over fashion you will likely end up carrying too much or wearing clothes that are uncomfortable.

Wearing uncomfortable shoes. This is actually the same point as above but, because it's your feet, it needed a separate entry. Nothing will ruin a trip faster than sore feet.

Holding to beauty routines that are unmanageable on the road. It is worth having easy hair options so your travel time is not consumed with such a mundane task as finding a salon for a color.

Arriving in a city in the dark. At night new places can look more ominous and make you anxious. Don't lose fun time with unnecessary doubts. Arrive during daylight.

Attracting unwanted attention. Expensive jewelry and revealing clothing can inadvertently attract attention from the wrong people. Adapt to your location.

Leaving valuables vulnerable. Choose a purse that you carry across your chest. Carry it with the opening next to your body and keep it zipped. In busy places, carry your daypack on your front and wrap your arm around it. Wear a money belt or use the hotel safe. Protect your valuables at all times.

Avoiding Culture Shock

The novelty of a new country is one of the great joys of travel – or the cause of serious culture shock.

It can be stressful when you don't know the language, exhausting when you can't accomplish the simplest of tasks and frustrating to be socially clumsy because you don't understand the culture. Here are a few tips to help you minimize the impact of culture shock.

Be knowledgeable: Research before you go. Read what you can about your destination: blogs, newspapers, even novels set in that location.

Be connected: Ask friends and family for a local contact. It's wonderful to receive a personal introduction to a new culture when you travel alone.

Be comfortable: Pack carefully to ensure that you have the appropriate clothes for your destination. You will feel more comfortable if you are properly dressed.

Be a chameleon: Watch carefully how people greet each other, how they line up for a bus, how they buy fruit. There are nuances in every aspect of a society. Look for them and adapt.

Be appropriately social: Observe how people interact in groups large and small, including where they stand, how they speak, where their eyes land.

Be respectful: Follow local customs to blend in and avoid difficult situations.

Be oriented: Start your visit with an overview of the city by taking a local tour. A walking tour will give you a close-up look at the culture but bus tours can be helpful for the bigger picture.

Be supported: Befriend your hotel desk clerk or coffee shop owner. Anyone you see on a regular basis can become your local go-to person for questions.

Be patient: If you are feeling culture shock, find a quiet place to relax and regroup.

14 Signs That You Have Had Too Much Alone Time

1... You've gone about as far as you can in learning to play the harmonica.

2... You've worn the same shirt across three borders but think: "well, it's new to them."

3... You step into a cab and "that smell" is you.

4... Your internal dialogue becomes your external dialogue.

5... Fingers become appropriate utensils for just about any occasion.

6... When you find an engaging conversation, the only response you can muster is "uh-huh."

7... You spend more than 20 minutes talking to your mugger – and he doesn't speak English.

9... You pretend to be lost just to talk to someone.

10... You see Sudoku when you close your eyes.

11... You sleep in your clothes.

12... You go to the hotel lobby in your pajamas.

13... When you speak, you only vaguely recognize your own voice.

14... You're so desperate to communicate in some way that you write a blog called Solo Traveler.

This was written by my son, Dylan, who did stand-up comedy in his teens. He just rattled these off. The last point was a gentle dig at me.

An organized tour can be great for solo travelers too.

Photo by Jane Okpala

Solo in a Group

Though I'm typically an independent solo traveler, I would like to dedicate some attention to groups for solo travelers. It can be the right choice for some people all of the time and for others some of the time.

The Pros and Cons of Packaged Travel
Solo travel can mean joining a group but not knowing anyone before you go. You might love this option. Here are the pros and cons:

Pros:

- The planning is done for you, including all the logistics and accommodation bookings.
- Language and cultural barriers are handled for you.
- You are sure to see the major sites.
- If things go wrong, someone else is responsible for setting them right.
- There is safety in numbers.
- You know that you'll have travel companions.
- You won't ever have to eat alone.

Cons:

- You may have to pay a single supplement (more on this soon).
- You will typically meet fewer locals and have fewer surprises (of the good kind).
- You may not see things off the beaten track.
- You can't save money on things that aren't important to you and splurge on things that are.
- You may be stuck with people you don't enjoy.
- You don't control your schedule.

Selecting the Tour that's Right for You

Whether your interest is adventure, culture, history, volunteering, shopping or walking, you'll find a tour company that fits your budget. But how do you decide which company is for you? Here are some guidelines:

- Review the itinerary carefully and compare it with other itineraries for the same destination: even those out of your price range. Once you know all the options, you'll be able to choose the tour that's right for you.
- Take note of what is and isn't included in the price, from transfers to meals. You want to know that you have enough money to really enjoy the trip.
- Know their refund policy.
- Look at the demographics of the group. Is this the group you want to travel with?
- Find out how large the group will be. Does this suit you?
- Is there a single supplement? Most package prices are based on double occupancy and some companies will charge a premium for singles. Find out if this is the case. Ask if they will waive it or pair you with another traveler to avoid the single supplement.
- Consider the reputation of the company. Look for reviews of the tour but also check with friends and use Facebook and Twitter to get firsthand feedback on the tour you're considering.
- Talk directly to the tour company to learn:
  - How the company is structured and whether they have people on the ground at your destination.
  - Whether the company is licensed to operate in your destination country.
  - How they choose their guides, what training the guides have and how they are accredited.
  - Their policies around sustainable tourism and buying local.

Solo Traveler on a Group Tour to Morocco
by Jane Okpala
20-something, New York City, USA

I usually backpack on my own, but for my trip to Morocco during Ramadan, I chose to join a tour. I absolutely loved it. I had the choice to wander off and do things on my own while still being able to be part of a small group and make friends. The biggest advantage to joining the group, though, was that it allowed me to engage in so many activities and cover so much of Morocco over the course of 2½ weeks. This would have been very difficult to arrange on my own.

During my trip, I visited the impressive Hassan II Mosque in Casablanca, smelled the tannery pits and observed rug weavers in the Fez medina, hiked into both the Atlas and Rif Mountains, caught a tagine cooking demonstration in Ait Benhaddou, explored a curio shop in Zagora that would make Indiana Jones proud, went sea kayaking in Essaouira, munched on a camel burger in Meknès, got scrubbed down to within an inch of my life at a hammam in Chefchaouen and watched snake charmers and belly dancers in Marrakech.

My two favorite places were Moulay Idriss, Morocco's holiest town and a beautiful, quiet place to truly experience a call to prayer during Ramadan, and Volubilis, where we had a fantastic local guide to lead us on a surprisingly non-boring walk through the Roman ruins and regale us with hilarious historical tidbits.

The absolute highlight of the trip for me was taking a camel ride into, and then camping out overnight in, the beautiful Sahara desert. We had tents, but most of us fell asleep under the sky near the campfire, listening to folk songs. Absolutely amazing.

Our group also took some time out for more conscious travel. We paid a visit to Project Horizon which is sponsored by Intrepid Travel. The center provides artificial limbs, wheelchairs, physical therapy, and job training to Moroccans with disabilities. We also spent some time at a women's argan oil collective learning about the various processes through which the argan nut is transformed into cooking and beauty products. At both of these stops, we had the opportunity to contribute to the work being done by making donations and/or buying some of the products made onsite.

The biggest recommendation I could give a solo traveler to Morocco would be to learn at least a few French phrases (assuming, of course, that you don't already know some Arabic). My French skills definitely came in handy when I was trying to get around or haggle for souvenirs.

Jane's solo tour through Morocco illustrates how taking a tour helps you see more of a country and culture than you might otherwise, while still going and seeing the world solo.

Beating the Single Supplement

Organized tours, cruises and resorts may be your travel choices. However, their price often includes the single supplement: the bane of solo travelers. The idea of paying more because you're only half of a couple seems counterintuitive and is frustrating, but it can be the economic reality. Here are a few strategies to beat it.

Google Alerts: When you start dreaming about a trip, create a Google Alert for your destination of choice and the term "single supplement waived". For example: Caribbean + resort + "single supplement waived". When a notice that the single supplement is waived at a Caribbean resort goes up on the web, you'll receive an e-mail alert from Google.

Ask: Speak directly with the tour company or use a travel agent who will go to bat for you. Either way, ask for the single supplement to be waived. Book your package far ahead of your departure date or wait until the last minute. The company may be willing to waive the supplement to kick off sales or sell off remaining spots. Of course, it helps if you're willing to walk away from the deal if you don't get what you want.

Pairing Up: Many tour companies will waive the single supplement if you're willing to share accommodation with another person of the same gender. In some cases, if they don't have a partner for you, they will still waive the single supplement.

Find a Travel Partner: If your preferred travel company doesn't offer a pairing service, you may find a travel partner through friends, Facebook or one of many specialty sites on the web. Simply search "find a travel partner" and you'll find many options. But don't go with just anyone. Be picky about who you'll spend your travel time with.

Go During the Shoulder Season: The off-season is usually "off" for a reason, but the shoulder season can be a spectacular time to travel. With fewer crowds it can be more enjoyable and you may be more successful in negotiating away the single supplement.

Negotiate an Upgrade: If you have to pay the full single supplement, maybe you can negotiate an upgrade on your room or what's included. It's always worth a try.

Find a Deal so Great…: If you find a screaming deal it just may be worth swallowing your solo pride and paying the single supplement.

LET THE ADVENTURE BEGIN

When you travel alone anything can happen.

You're open to the world.
And the world is open to you.

Kissed on the Blues Highway

Like a kiss, the blues can be gentle and sweet or wild and passionate. On my trip down Highway 61, the Blues Highway, I was kissed both ways by the blues.

What do I know about the blues? Not a whole lot. I know the majors like Sonny Terry & Brownie McGhee; my brother introduced me to them as a teenager. I know Buddy Guy; my husband and I saw him in Atlanta. And of course, there is B.B. King; he actually did kiss me. But that part of the story comes later.

The fact is I don't know a lot but, when it comes to the blues, you don't need to know it; you just need to feel it.

Life in 12 Bars

This trip had a blues theme. After all, I started in Chicago and traveled to New Orleans visiting as many blues bars as I could. I had wanted to take this trip for many years.

Why? I kept asking myself this question. The only answer I could muster is that there is a magical quality to the blues. A mythology around its origins. A simplicity that invites anyone interested to enter and enjoy.

And just as the blues' 12-bar progression has a certain predictability, so does life. And as the tunes share common themes, so do we all. We all live, love, grieve, and experience joy and heartbreak. I don't know any other form of music so pure. I guess I was looking for the heart of the blues.

Solo is not Blue

Many of the people I met on this trip were surprised by my choice to travel solo. They thought I might be lonely and sad. But I wasn't. I've been those things. I've been blue but not due to traveling alone.

As I traveled down the Blues Highway, I sought out the best blues I could find. Eddie Shaw at Kingston Mines in Chicago and the house band at B.B. King's in Memphis were great. I really enjoyed Jeff Greenberg at Jimbeaux's in New Orleans. But for me, the best was in Jackson, Mississippi at 930 Blues Cafe. There I thrilled to Jackson's Blues Sweetheart, Jackie Bell – a stunning singer and an equally amazing performer.

At 930 Blues I met Herbert, Isaac the club owner, and Marvin who worked security. As a single woman, I felt wonderfully safe and happy that night. Even as I stepped into the cab to go back to my hotel, Marvin looked the driver right in the eye and said: "You take care of my friend, y'hear." Safe. Totally safe.

Then there's B.B., the King of the Blues

I guess I really fell in love with the blues the night I went to a small club under the boardwalk in Redondo Beach, California. That boardwalk, along with the club, is long gone but not my memory of seeing B.B. there. The venue was small and somewhat sophisticated as I remember. Cabaret style. B.B. played long sets. At one point a string broke on his guitar and he continued to play as he restrung it. Later in the evening, he offered the women pins of his famed guitar, Lucille.

Shy as I was back then, I was the last woman to make my way forward to get a pin. He looked at me. He had no more. So he leaned in and kissed me on my left cheek.

Oh yes, I've been kissed by the blues.

The Social Side of Solo – Alone but Not Lonely

My fondest travel memories are always of the people I meet along the way.

In the solo travel stories peppered throughout this book you meet many of them. Yet, there are countless other people whose company I've enjoyed on my travels: sometimes for a few minutes, sometimes for a few hours. Here are a few of my favorites.

Patagonia, Chile On the Navimag Ferry on my way to Patagonia to hike in Torres del Paine I met many solo travelers. One of the special ones was Noemie, from France. She has a powerful energy and we struck up an immediate friendship. Within a day we were making plans to camp and hike Patagonia together. She made a magical trip even more so.

Orlando Airport, Florida, USA On my way to speak at a conference in Florida, I made a whirlwind yet substantial connection with Rick at the Orlando Airport. We exchanged travel stories and life stories. He eventually contributed a post to Solo Traveler about volunteering on the Camino de Santiago. We continue to stay in touch via e-mail.

Park City, Utah, USA I first met Olivia on Facebook: we were both going to Park City to volunteer at the Sundance Film Festival. To my surprise, without planning, she was the first person I met when I got there. We kept running into each other. It was extraordinary but not surprising given our mutual interests and enthusiasm for taking in as much of the event as we could.

Ambleside, Lake District, UK I met many people at the Unicorn Inn over the four days I was in Ambleside. It was amazing. On my last evening, when I entered the bar I was greeted like a long-tme friend. I couldn't pay for a beer to save my life that night. Such hospitality.

Truly, it's the people I meet who make my travels so wonderful.

How to Meet Locals and Other Travelers

So how do you connect with such wonderful people as you travel? Here's how I do it.

- Choose your accommodation wisely. Hostels and B&Bs are naturally more social than hotels.
- Consider traveling by train. The dining, bar and observation cars are great places to meet people.
- Take advantage of volunteer tour organizations like Big Apple Greeters in New York City. You will often find them through tourist bureau websites and many are free. Use Google to search "free walking tour and (your destination city)". These tours are found all over the world, particularly in Europe, and the guides (often local college students) merely ask for tips if you enjoyed your tour. There are also excellent local tour companies in just about every destination.
- Take classes to learn a language or new culinary skills – whatever interests you. You'll meet a group of people who share your interest.
- Go to restaurants with communal tables and coffee shops that are freelancer hubs.
- When you are in one place for a while, go to the same market, flower shop or restaurant consistently. You'll be noticed as a new regular and people will eventually chat with you.
- If you're long-term traveling, break up the trip with an organized tour. You'll enjoy the company and a chance to let someone else take charge for a while.
- Learn how to talk to strangers.

How to Talk to Strangers

It might be easy to conclude that solo travel is for gregarious, outgoing people. But the truth is, shy people enjoy traveling alone as well and there's something about being away, out of the norm of everyday life, that helps even shy people stretch and talk to strangers.

While there are a number of ways to start conversations, the best is your smile. A warm smile tells people that you are friendly and safe. But here are some starters for specific situations:

Locals: Start with a question that allows them to share their love and knowledge of their city or community. Or ask those preparing a meal (street food vendors, guesthouse owners) what goes into it. People are happy to talk about their own hard work and it shows you care about the destination when you are curious to learn more about it.

Other solo travelers: You'll recognize solo travelers by the place settings at a table or the solo seat on a tour. But just because they're alone, don't assume that they want company. Open with something easy like a comment about the weather and see if they take the conversation further.

Other tourists: Chatting with a couple or small group of tourists can be fun too. Look for the person in the group who is gregarious but not the organizer: the latter is too busy being responsible. Just ask where they're from and the conversation has begun.

In a club: Sit at the bar. This is more social than a table. Comment on the band and ask about the music scene in town. It will be obvious that you are a tourist, which makes you interesting.

Anywhere: If you are really, really curious about something, spot a person you'd like to speak with and ask your question. There is nothing better than genuine curiosity to engage people. And master the art of the follow-up question. Ask "why" and "how" questions that lend themselves to open conversations. People love talking about their city, themselves, their thoughts and knowledge.

"Tell Me Your Story"

When it is clear that you'll be spending some time with someone new – either on a tour or sharing a meal - ask them for their story. Everyone has a story but how often do people get to tell it? People love it and they open up.

66 *Solo travel allows me to reconnect with and resurrect someone I thought I had lost.* 99

Saralee R. Leary
50-something, Rhode Island, USA
photo in email.

Noemie and I met on the Navimag Ferry then hiked and camped together in Torres del Paine National Park – Patagonia, Chile.

Meeting Jamie Steel: The Man About Town

He was due for his annual hair cut. Yes, his white hair was past his shoulders and his beard was down to his chest. Definitely a character. I walked up to him and said: "Mr. Steel, I understand that you're the person I have to meet." He was somewhat surprised but not really taken aback. He seemed to know that he was the unofficial cultural liaison for St. Andrews by-the-Sea, New Brunswick.

Jamie Steel is the type of person I look for in every small town I visit. He is one of the reasons small towns make great destinations. He's an outlier, a person who stands apart from others in some distinct way. Jamie is exceptional for his role in the music scene. The important characters of other towns may stand out for their age, the stories they tell or their unofficial political role. These are people really worth knowing but you rarely bump into them. They are typically found through others by accident. I find them by simply asking.

The shopkeeper of Kilt & Kaboodle told me about Jamie Steel. "Who is the person in town that I just have to meet?" I asked. My assumption is that the person I find to chat with easily – the chance encounter in a coffee shop or a clerk at a Visitor Information Center – is not the most interesting person in town, but that they know who is. So I ask.

She thought about it for just a moment and then said "Jamie Steel."

"Where would I find him?"

She stepped out of the shop to point out the pub I should go to that evening and there he was, walking in, at that very moment.

Off I went and, as I told you, I walked right up to him and introduced myself. And what good fortune that I did. Jamie Steel is not only the Executive Director of the Sunbury Shores Arts & Nature Centre but he also books the musical talent in the town. He invited me back to the pub that evening to see Adam Olmstead, a local boy who made good in Nashville and was on his way through town to play at a festival in Nova Scotia. He would play at the pub that night with the Nashville String Band, a band that includes a number of Grammy Award-winning members.

I returned after dinner that evening, listened to the music and met the entire band. I don't usually play the groupie but this was a fabulous night! We don't always meet the Jamie Steels of the world but we have a better chance of doing so if we actively look for them. How fortunate I was to meet Jamie in St. Andrews by-the-Sea.

Meeting people like Jamie Steel is one of the great pleasures of solo travel – St. Andrews by-the-Sea, New Brunswick.

Sharing Special Moments

The amazing sunset. The inspiring play. The vibrant market scene. It can be frustrating not to have someone to share special moments with when traveling alone. Here are a few ways to get past this issue.

Find a temporary travel mate. Whether for a couple of hours or a few days, solo travelers connect with temporary travel mates all the time. You can meet them at hostels or B&Bs. It's a great way to share travels without a long-term commitment. If you've rented a car, others may be willing to chip in on the cost and share the adventure.

Use your smart phone. Send photos to friends at home the moment they are taken and then chat about them via Skype.

Join a short-term tour. Whether it's a one-hour tour of a museum or a weekend rafting, you can join a group and share the experience with others – then say ta-ta.

Engage the people around you spontaneously. Take a picture of your food, notice the fantastic dessert at the table beside you and smile at the person about to eat it or make an off-hand comment. There are many ways to start a conversation.

Write a personal travel blog. Writing a travel blog to share with friends and family is free and easy. See options in the resources section at the back of this book.

Master the art of the self-portrait. Don't forget to take photos of yourself on your travels. Friends get bored of scenery shots but they're happy to see photos of you in exotic places. See the section on Self-portrait Photography.

Play with social media. Use Facebook and Twitter to share your experiences in quick, easy and frequent snippets. Instagram, Pinterest and Foodspotting are becoming popular too.

Offer yourself as a photographer. Ask someone taking a picture if they would like you to take it for them. Then ask for the favor returned. You're not doing this so much for the photo as the chance to talk about the experience you are sharing.

Finding Solitude When You Want It

It's probably clear by now that I really like meeting people when I travel. However, some solo travelers go alone to be alone. They are looking for solitude and it can be hard to find.

Here are a few ideas to stave off helpful advice and kind invitations. Here's how to find solitude when traveling solo:

- Go places where solitude is respected: parks, galleries, museums and libraries.
- Look lost in your own thoughts.
- Don't make eye contact with people.
- Act capable and confident.
- Turn your back to the room in coffee shops and restaurants.
- On a tour, sit in the middle of the bus. Enthusiasts are at the front, people making their own party are at the back.
- Absorb yourself in a book or your diary. If you prefer sketching, you may need to employ some of the techniques above as people often feel free to have a look.
- Look grumpy.
- Have the confidence to say that you want to be alone.
- Wear headphones. Even if your music is silent, no one knows that but you.

A Table for One: Restaurants and Meals

Eating alone. Yes, this is one of the biggest concerns people have when they think about traveling solo. But it needn't be an issue. There are many ways to eat alone and feel fine about it and there are also ways to go to a restaurant alone and end up eating with new friends. Here are a few ideas:

Freelance Hubs: Look for independent coffee shops that are used as alternative offices by freelancers. These are places of community. They have a good vibe, they tend to be off the beaten path, they don't rush customers out the door and they usually have free Wi-Fi. They are also great places for a light meal.

Restaurants with Communal Tables: Some are casual, some are upscale; there are all kinds of restaurants with communal tables. You just have to look for them. Communal tables can be great for meeting people, chatting, laughing and learning firsthand about a city or neighborhood.

Restaurants with Bars: Eating at the bar leaves you open for conversation with the bartender if no one else. But I usually do meet other people. In Havana I happened to be reading a very funny book and discovered that when you laugh out loud while reading a book showing an English title, you'll be talking to people in no time.

Pubs or Casual Restaurants: The tables are closer together in these places, which makes them great for chatting with people, especially after you've taken a photo of your food. This always attracts attention. Offer a smile in return and a conversation will begin.

Tourist Traps: If you're feeling lonely for home, tourist traps are the places to go. Everyone at these restaurants is from away and many will speak English.

Picnics: Buy food at a local supermarket or take-out restaurant and eat in a park.

Find Other Solo Diners: Ask the host or hostess whether there is another solo diner who they think would like company or scan the restaurant yourself for a likely person. You can invite them to join you. I haven't been turned down yet.

The Classic: Bring a book or write postcards.

---

66 *I love traveling. Period. However, I was always rather hesitant about traveling alone. It's probably got to do with the fact that I've never liked eating alone. So, when I embarked on a solo five-month round-the-world trip in 2008, I was terribly excited but I was also a bit doubtful that I would enjoy it. I had travelled alone before but never for such a lengthy amount of time.*

I can tell you this now: within the first week, those doubts had evaporated into thin air! I had the best time of my life: I learned a slew of new things about myself, about our world and its people and about being a more open-minded, balanced and positive individual. Since that trip, I've become a solo travel 'convert. 99

Keith Jenkins
30-something, Amsterdam, The Netherlands
VelvetEscape.com/blog

I was eating a cricket - never again! – Hacienda Tres Rios, Mexico.

Evenings with More than a Book

At home, you may not go out alone at night. But if you do, there are likely only a limited number of places you would go. Maybe a movie is okay but a pub isn't. After all, you have friends to go to a pub with and it's uncomfortable to look like you are on your own in a bar.

Traveling solo, everything changes. While you don't have those friends as companions, you do have two things on your side:

- Your need to explore the city at night.
- The fact that, as a solo traveler, you are fascinating.

Yes, people will find you interesting simply because you are a traveler and, apparently, an intrepid one at that. So get out there and explore. Great choices for an evening out include:

- Festivals, whether they are cultural, food or music.
- Pubs where the locals hang out.
- Restaurants with communal tables.
- The theater, opera, symphony, ballet.
- Bars with live music.
- Hostels and guesthouses that often have evening events.

How to Find the Right Place

I start looking for the right place for evenings before I get into town by reading recommendations on blogs and guides. But I don't assume that I've found it. More than half the time I change my mind after talking to a taxi driver, bartender or server in a restaurant. In other words, I find the best places by talking to locals and being flexible.

Pubbing and Clubbing

You can have a great night on the town alone. I've been to blues bars, dance clubs, local pubs and, with few exceptions, had a fantastic time meeting people and enjoying the night life. But going out to a club or pub alone successfully requires a slightly different approach than doing so at home with friends. Take these tips:

Getting There

- Don't carry a purse. Leave valuables in the hotel safe or use your money belt for most money, credit cards, passport, etc.. Have some money in different pockets for drinks.
- Dress conservatively for the culture.
- If there's a huge lineup outside a club and you're feeling a bit uneasy about going in alone, find someone in line who looks really safe. Look for the quieter people or an older couple – people who are not out to make the biggest party of the night – and approach them as if they are old friends so that others don't object to you cutting in. Then explain that you are alone

and would like to join them just until you get inside. They'll understand that you need a bit of safety. Once inside, you can make a graceful exit from them – or you may have made new friends.

- If it's a small place, arrive early so that you have your choice as to where to sit.

Once Inside

- Sit at the bar. It's more social at the bar and you'll be sitting physically higher than most people in the room, giving you a good view for safety.
- Alternatively, choose a seat with a good vantage point. Pubs often have bench seats with tables along two walls. Sit on the short side of this "L" configuration. It's like sitting at the head of a table. You are in a position of power and have access to more people for chatting.
- Make friends with your bartender or server. They'll notice you're alone and take care of you in case of unwanted attention.
- Notice where the exits are. If anything goes wrong you want out fast.
- Choose who you want to talk to and go for it. By being proactive you prevent the wrong person from monopolizing your evening and you'll have a great time with the right people.
- Never drink too much. In fact, drink far less than you would if you were at home. You want to have all your faculties about you to deal with any surprising situations.

Plan Your Exit

- If you have made friends, plan your exit. However nice they may seem, don't accept a ride from them. Get a taxi. This may require leaving early or after them. You can also discreetly ask staff to call you a taxi so that when an offer of a ride does come you have other arrangements.

Havana, Hungarians and a Salsa Club

A pub, yes. Clubbing, not so much. But I had heard that this one club in Havana was really worth it. So, off I went, not knowing how I was going to manage it.

La Casa de la Música de Centro Habana is one of the city's most popular salsa clubs. It's very large and attracts some of the best bands in the country and hundreds of locals every night. When I went, I saw only three obvious tourists in a massive lineup. It made the idea of entering the club solo a bit intimidating. So, I approached those tourists as if they were long lost friends and joined the line.

Unfortunately, my new companions were Hungarian. They barely spoke a word of English. Fortunately, they eventually understood that I was on my own and wanted to join them, at least until I got in the door and sussed out the situation. They were quite accommodating.

Inside, I decided to stick with them despite the language barrier. I still wasn't comfortable. And then I had the greatest of luck. Their local tour guide caught up with them. Exhausted from a day of strained communication, he practically leapt across the table when he realized that I spoke English.

We had a great night. The band was fabulous. The dance floor was a spectacle. And the guide taught me how to salsa.

Sex and the Solo Traveler

Some people wouldn't consider having sex with someone they've just met, but others would. While I don't recommend it, I would like to address the topic.

First the cautionary notes:

- You don't know a stranger. And anyone you've just met — whether it's been an hour, a day or a bit longer — is a stranger. You don't know their values. You don't know their motives. Even if all seems great, they could be playing you. By finding a private place for sex you are putting yourself in danger.
- Whether you speak the language or not, you are in another culture and you won't be able to read the behavior of that enticing person properly. You are out of your element. Assume that your judgment is poor.
- You have no back up: no friends in the area or family to call. You have no one who knows this person to confirm that they are safe.
- Disease contracted through sex is a souvenir you don't want.

It may not be much fun but it is likely a good idea: learn how to say no. Abstinence is definitely the safest choice! But, if after assessing the situation with a somewhat clear head, and within the cautionary notes above, you decide to go for it, please do so safely. Here are a few safety tips:

- Let someone responsible know where you are going. Don't be shy. Text a friend or tell the desk clerk. And let your prospective partner be aware that you are doing so. There is nothing like being seen to increase safety.
- Be aware of the diseases you can contract sexually and how to protect yourself.
- Women should consider carrying and maintaining their birth control regime and/or the morning after pill while traveling if you plan to engage in sex.
- If you have engaged in unsafe sex, go to a clinic to be tested for disease. Women should take a pregnancy test.

Temptation! Yes, it can be tempting sometimes to get involved with someone when traveling, but for the sake of your health and your life, play it safe.

Solo Road Trips

I love road trips! Driving music, the open road and the opportunity to change the itinerary on a moment's notice are wonderful. But going solo there are a few details that need your attention.

Make sure you have:

- Roadside assistance. Have a membership to AAA, CAA or some other roadside assistance program.
- A cell phone with good coverage and an adapter so that you can charge it in the car.
- An emergency safety kit that has some non-perishable food, distilled water, blanket, first aid kit, beeswax candle, matches, wind-up flashlight, a whistle and flares.
- A GPS. It's not always accurate on highways but in the city it can be exceptionally helpful, especially with one-way streets.
- A good map. Since a GPS isn't always right and you may want to deviate from its preferred route, it's good to have a map.
- A compass. I find that, despite having a pretty good sense of direction, I sometimes get nervous that I have gone too far, missed an exit or simply taken the wrong ramp. A compass is useful as it lets you know at least that you're going in the right direction. Most smartphones today have compasses. If yours doesn't, download an app for one.
- Your tongue in your mouth. Whenever I was late with a lame excuse, my mother would say "you have a tongue in your mouth, don't you?" The ability to ask questions is essential on any road trip.

Fun extras to bring on a solo road trip:
- Loaded MP3 player.
- A list of awesomely tacky roadside tourist attractions.
- Easy snacks to eat on the road.
- Fun cameras or apps with photo effects for your phone.
- List of any CouchSurfing events or Meetups happening while you pass through a town.

For some, a car is simply transportation. For others it's freedom.
That's how I feel on a road trip – Prince Edward County, Ontario.

Travel Solo for a Rocky Mountain High

It was a stunning day in Park City, Utah. Perfect for skiing. Unfortunately, my day got turned upside down. I had planned to be on the slopes at 9:00 a.m. but a meeting got in the way and I didn't make it until noon. "Okay," I thought. "I can get in a run or two before heading to town to catch a couple of films." Ah, but fate had other plans. Good plans.

Being mid-week and during the Sundance Film Festival, the ski hill was not busy at all. The sky was an incredible blue. The air was crisp but not chilling. It was a cozy cold. Cold enough to keep the snow dry and your face warm. Going up the gondola by myself I felt full of joy. I actually laughed out loud with delight. This was different from the pleasure of seeing interesting films. This was exhilarating. This was fun.

Given how little time I had, I thought I wouldn't eat but another couple thousand feet in altitude made me think twice. I headed into the Red Pine Lodge at the top of the gondola to grab a bit of lunch.

In the cafeteria line I had a few passing words with a man named Philip. We went in different directions and then met again at the checkout. While the cashier made the suggestion, we decided it was a bit early in our relationship for him to buy me lunch.

We met again at the condiments counter and, as we both scanned the sea of people to find a table, we decided to eat lunch together. Lunch turned into an afternoon of skiing. And what an afternoon!

Philip was a much better skier than me. Fortunately, he was a patient man. He politely took all blue square runs (my comfort level) and skied up the sides and through the trees when the opportunity presented itself. If we were sure that a black diamond and a blue square connected, he took the former and we met at the bottom.

He had the map and, I suspect, he studied it while he waited for me. He guided us run after run so that we never covered one twice. It was fantastic!

And our timing was perfect too. The lifts closed at 4pm and we climbed on for the last ride up at 3:57. We skied all the way to the base, getting in every possible skiing minute we could. What a fantastic day!

Taking a break from the Sundance Film Festival to go skiing at The Canyons – Park City, Utah.

Long-Term Solo Travel

Traveling for an extended period of time uses many of the same skills as short solo trips but it does warrant some special attention. You will need to go at a slower pace. You can't travel with the same intensity for a few months as you do for a couple of weeks. This is good because you'll get to know the places you visit on a deeper level.

When planning a long-term trip, consider:

- Regular communication. You may not focus on connecting with home when you're traveling for a short time but on a long trip this will mean a lot to you. Plus, for safety's sake, someone should always be aware of your next move. Skype can be free with a computer or smartphone and Internet access, or look into Google Voice, which more easily allows you to dial cell phones if you qualify for an account.
- Renting an apartment for a longer stay once in a while. It will help you feel more settled. It can also make economic sense.
- Building something into your routine that is familiar to you, something you typically do at home. It could be painting, reading, cooking, etc.
- Using the local library. There may be an English section. You may even be able to get a card.
- Going to the same coffee shop, market or restaurant a number of times to get to know a few of the locals.
- Treating yourself to a small bouquet of flowers or a spa day or a fine scotch. Do something special just for you.
- Exploring the expat situation or meetup.com as a way to make friends.
- Taking a job. Google "travel jobs abroad" for websites with some unique opportunities for travelers.
- How you're going to manage your money and postal mail. It may be helpful to have a trusted friend or family member at home to take care of your bills and move money around when necessary.
- Keeping a healthy lifestyle. Eat well, drink lots of water and get an adequate amount of sleep. Covering all the basics of a healthy lifestyle is more important on long trips than short.

- Picking up a tour and letting someone else take care of all the travel details for a while.
- Taking the train or bus so that you see the countryside and really get a sense of the geography.
- Importing some comfort food. E-mail home and ask for a care package of your favorite cereal or cookies that you haven't had for a while.
- Inviting friends to join you for periods of time.
- Joining a local running, wine tasting or reading group.

Self-portrait Photography

Capturing the moment in photographs is as important to solo travelers as it is to anyone. And while it's fine that we're not in most of the shots, it would be nice to have the occasional photo as evidence that we were actually there.

But there are hazards to taking your own photo. With most cameras you can't look through the viewfinder and take your photo at the same time. And when using a camera with an articulating screen, I find myself looking at the screen rather than into the lens with less than satisfactory results.

Fortunately, with a bit of practice, you can take great self-portraits by mastering the one-handed, no viewfinder shot. Here's how:

- Use the widest angle your camera offers. Zooming in leaves too little room for error.
- Extend your arm fully out front and to the side by about 35 degrees. This should put you and your background into the shot.
- Raise your arm up from shoulder height; we all look better in photos taken slightly from above.
- Through hit and miss, discover the best angle to show your best side.
- Use that same angle whenever possible.
- Make sure that there are no smokestacks or flowerpots positioned behind your head (so that they don't appear to be springing out of your head in the photo).

- Be aware of the location of the sun to avoid ghastly shadows under the eyes or the silhouette effect.
- Don't be shy to send a big smile into the camera. So what if people around are looking at you oddly. You're happy and your photos should reflect that.
- Delete all horrible pictures of you.

The iPhone/Android Option

Many phones have fantastic cameras and the ability not only to shoot what's in front of you but also to shoot you while you're looking at the screen. I still prefer my camera because it offers a wider lens and better quality, however, in a pinch the phone is a great solution.

The one-handed self-portrait is an important skill for the solo traveler to develop.
– Toronto, Canada

Home is Where Your Heart Is

Over the years, my husband and I traveled many places: just the two of us at times, other times with the kids. Traveling together, we often fell in love with the places we visited. We could imagine living there. We would consider living there. From small prairie towns to the south of France, from California to Scotland, this happened.

One morning on a solo trip around Lake Ontario, I woke up in Prince Edward County, Canada. This is an absolutely wonderful place. It has fine wine, fantastic food and great art, along with a rolling landscape, country roads, lake views and beaches. This is a place where my husband and I would have considered living.

At that moment I realized that, without him, I was not considering this. It had been possible to think about living elsewhere because I used to travel with my heart; the primary love of my life was with me. Home could be anywhere we were together.

But now that's not the case. I travel solo and the love in my life resides in Toronto where three of my children live, my Mom and my siblings and their families, friends and neighbors — it is these people who now collectively hold my heart.

They are my home.

SAFETY TRUMPS EVERYTHING

It's simple: safety does trump everything.

This section looks at preventive safety strategies: ways to help you avoid dangerous situations and people. Please read it carefully but keep in mind that it is impossible to cover every situation and circumstance you will encounter. Your safety is ultimately up to you.

Caught in a Con Game in Paris

This is a story of firsts. My first time in Europe. My first solo travel adventure long before my marriage and my incarnation as a travel blogger. And my first – and last – time being caught in a con game. It was 1985, I was 27 and I really should have known better.

My trip began in Paris where I spent my time bopping around the city with fellow hostellers, both men and women. I felt safe and confident. On the day I was to leave for Salzburg, I felt the same way. I was to take an afternoon train so I stored my backpack in a locker at the Gare de L'Est around noon, then went across the street to look over a menu outside a restaurant. A man approached and checked it out as well. We chatted and went in to spend lunch together. No big deal. Meeting and hanging out with people in Paris seemed normal at this point.

While we were eating, a man at another table leaned over and asked for a light for his cigarette. The fellow I was with (let's call him John) provided it and we all got chatting. It turned out that we were all heading to different cities in Austria.

The other man (I'll call him Peter) got up to leave and casually mentioned that he had to pop into a bank to pick up the Austrian schillings required to enter Austria. This was before Euros and was news to me. Assuming that this was a detail I missed, I joined the two men and went to get my money changed.

The bank we went to couldn't change our money. It is only with hindsight that I realize that it was likely a commercial bank. I didn't even know of their existence then. From this point onwards, my trip took a very dangerous trajectory, one that fortunately ended well. My choices at each step may suggest that I was a stupid woman but I wasn't. I was, however, very naive.

A con game is all about gaining the confidence of the mark: in this case, me. The end objective is different with every con artist but the process is pretty well the same: prey on a human frailty such as vanity, greed or naiveté, gain the person's confidence, and then get what you want from them. The thrill of the con is often as important as the results.

After being unsuccessful at the bank, the three of us set out for an Austrian restaurant which John knew. He was sure that the owner would exchange our money so that we could continue our travels. We positioned ourselves at a café across the street from the restaurant. I went to the restroom and took money out of my money belt, went back to the table and gave it to him. Peter gave him cash as well.

As John entered the restaurant across the street, Peter asked how long we had been traveling together. To his apparent shock, I said we weren't travel mates, and that I had just met him.

"But, you're my insurance," he said.

We both sat back and waited anxiously to see if our money was lost. However, John returned, explained that he had not been successful and gave our money back.

Confidence earned.

We then went to another Austrian restaurant on the Champs-Elysées and repeated the process. This time John returned with Peter's money exchanged but there had not been enough for both of us. Again, he gave me back my money.

Confidence confirmed.

Peter wished us luck and continued on his way. John and I then headed for the Left Bank where we would try once again. I know. You're thinking how crazy I was but it actually seemed pretty realistic. They were pros!

The day was getting on. This time when John went to get the money exchanged he returned and said he had to leave it at the restaurant, but that we could return in an hour to get it. Naturally this made me anxious but there was little I could do. We went for dinner across the street to wait it out.

At dinner John mentioned that we had missed the train and would have to stay overnight; we could share a room. At this proposal I certainly drew the line. I refused and he got angry. When I moved to leave he settled down. After doing this dance a couple of times, I pulled out a photo of my two-year-old son. He looked at me, stunned.

"How old are you?"

It was not a good scene. I left him and looked for a phone booth to call a remote connection I had in the city. The booth was occupied. I knocked. I got the one minute hand signal and the person's back. I looked and saw John watching me. I went to the other side of the booth and pounded on it furiously. The man eventually left in a huff and I called. Once it was clear that I was talking to someone I knew, John took off: with my money, of course.

Long story short, I grabbed a cab and went to my contact's home. She said that had John been successful, I would have been en route for the white slave market. Is that the case? I'm not sure. But I certainly wasn't going on any holiday.

The details of that day are indelibly marked in my memory. What saved me was the fact that I stayed in a public place. While I was significantly poorer in the end, I was left with my life and with a lifelong principle for solo travel: public is always safer than private.

That trip lasted another seven days. I crisscrossed Europe by train as far as Budapest in the east and Amsterdam to the north, and many points in between. As I did, I told the story to as many women as possible.

Travel with the Wit of an Adult
And the Wonder of a Child

In 2007, Joshua Bell, one of America's most amazing violinists, played in the subway in Washington, D.C. on a violin handcrafted by Antonio Stradivari in 1713 – an instrument that Bell had bought several years earlier for a reported $3.5 million.

He was almost completely ignored by the passersby. People pay dearly to attend one of his concerts, yet few stopped to enjoy his beautiful music. They walked through the subway with blinders on.

Being open to that which is beautiful is important. Being safe and not engaging with just anyone is also important.

See what is in front of you. Be on your guard if necessary but let your guard down at times. Tap into the wonder you had as a child when you knew immediately whether you liked or disliked something. You didn't need a price tag to tell you what you valued then, and you shouldn't now.

Three solo travelers join up for a safari. Wit and wonder in play – Rajiji National Park , India.

The Four Priorities of Safety

What matters:

Your person.

Your documents.

Your money.

Your stuff.

In that order.

The Five Principles of Safety

When I traveled solo in my twenties, I was on autopilot. I did what came naturally and, with a bit of luck, it all worked out.

Now, as a more mature adult and a blogger, I take time to reflect on what I do and how I do it. If you remember none of the tips that follow this section, I hope that you will remember these five principles.

Solo Travel Principle #1: Public is safer than private.

This is my number one rule: stay in busy, public places. Regardless of how comfortable you are with a new acquaintance, going to a private place with them can put you in a dangerous situation. Even a taxi should be considered private as you don't necessarily know whether the driver and the acquaintance are in cahoots. So think of public as truly public; places where you are in control.

Solo Travel Principle #2: Proactive is better than reactive.

Imagine yourself in a bar or train station. You have a question or you want to meet someone and have a chat. In situations like this it's better to be proactive than reactive because it's more likely that an inappropriate person will choose you than you will choose him or her. Enjoy the unique social opportunities that solo travel presents but do so on your terms and stay safe.

Solo Travel Principle #3: People can be engaged in your safety.

When you are walking to a destination but no longer sure of your safety, stop and ask directions even if you know the way. People will redirect you if you're headed into an unsafe area. If you go to a nightclub to take in some music, connect with the bartender or a security guard so that they are aware that you're alone. They'll watch out for you and move unwanted attention away. Whenever possible, engage others in your safety.

Solo Travel Principle #4: Decisions should not be rushed.

The easiest way to be conned or ripped off is to be rushed into a decision. This is a common strategy of people who want to take you for more than they should. It usually starts with introducing new, credible, but inaccurate information that requires you to make a decision quickly. Don't. Get yourself in a safe place to decide on your terms.

Solo Travel Principle #5: Being rude can offer protection.
I am sure that you are typically polite and congenial with everyone you meet. After all, it makes for a happier life. However, when it comes to safety, if polite doesn't work, allow yourself to be rude – especially when traveling solo. Regardless of whether it may hurt someone's feelings or disturb other people, if you have to, be rude to ensure your safety.

One further note:
There is a gender bias around safety. Men are often considered to be more dangerous than women but this is not necessarily true. There are dangerous women who are just as capable of luring you into bad situations as men. Be aware of this.

These principles are important but please read the safety tips as well.

Public (like a busy subway) is safer than private. And sometimes you get the added bonus of performance art like I did this time in Moscow.

Who Are the Most Hospitable People in the World?

Who are the most hospitable people in the world?

No one can answer this question definitively but if asked to put forth a nomination, I'd suggest the warm people of India. I could support this with many stories but here I will offer three.

"Come to my brother's wedding."

Before leaving for India, I met Jackie, the owner of India Village Restaurant in Ancaster, Ontario. As I was finishing my dinner with a friend she came to join us at our table. It wasn't long into our conversation about my upcoming trip that she stopped everything and asked me to join her on her trip home to her brother's wedding. I accepted the invitation immediately. What an opportunity and what hospitality!

We flew into Delhi. After a three-hour drive to Jackie's home town of Ahmedgarh, we arrived in the middle of a pre-wedding party. The back lane to their house had been transformed into a disco: dance floor, loud Indian music and all. I was grabbed by the young girls to dance with them. Next, I was taken upstairs so that Jackie and her sisters could decide what I would wear to the wedding the following day. I was given a beautiful pink suit. But there was more: I had to have my arms hennaed for the wedding. Sleep? It was possible only around 2:00 a.m. and we were up for 6:00 to be ready to leave two hours later.

For the next four days I enjoyed hospitality at every turn. I was treated like royalty and could not lift a finger to help. I met neighbors and relatives. I celebrated with them and enjoyed the banter and cajoling of the family without understanding a word.

After telling this story to others, I have learned that it is not uncommon at all to be invited to an Indian wedding despite not knowing the family. Everyone is welcome. That's hospitality!

"But you are our guest!"

"But you are our guest" is a statement that I heard frequently in India. Indians are generous and hospitable and they show it in many ways.

On a train between Pushkar and Udaipur I was traveling with a woman from the UK. Our seats were separated by one row so, as is common in India, I moved into the single seat beside her, knowing that the single person who was assigned it would be just as happy with the one assigned to me. And he was.

However, when he went to claim my seat a woman was sitting there who refused to move. I'm sure he would have been happy to sit in her seat except that it was on another car so he could not get to it. I stood up to help but the young man refused. "You are our guest. Please sit down. I will take care of this," he said.

Well, despite getting the conductor involved, the woman did not move. I am sure that if I was the one out of my seat the conductor would have made arrangements for both of us but the young man would not allow me to get involved. As a result, the young man stood between the cars for the entire trip.

Adopted on an Overnight Train

Like bookends to my trip, my final twenty-four hours in India featured hospitality similar to my first twenty-four. I was leaving Rathambore on the overnight train to Delhi. On the platform, waiting for the train at the exact location where my car would arrive, I met Madhu and Harpreet, sisters-in-law who had enjoyed a weekend getaway together.

After chatting and exchanging our stories, the train arrived. By that time, I was adopted. They helped me find my berth, made sure that I got all the linens I needed and even made my bed for me. I texted a friend back home that "I had landed in the arms of angels."

In the morning, our train pulled into Delhi at 5:00 a.m. and, because I had had no Internet access for six days, I didn't have any arrangements for my arrival. My backup plan was simply to stick it out in the train station until a reasonable hour for exploring the city — but that was unnecessary. I went with Madhu and Harpreet and their driver to the home of Madhu. I felt completely safe but I texted my friend again with the address just to be on the safe side. I was given tea and a bed was made for me to have a nap. At 9:00 a.m., they woke me for breakfast. We enjoyed chatting and learning about each other. Then they found a driver for me for the day. I went out and saw Delhi before going to the airport that night.

Such extraordinary hospitality.

On the Ground Safety

There are places in the world where there is unrest. Violence happens and I would never recommend that a solo traveler go to an unsafe destination. I am not that adventurous myself, so I'm not inclined to suggest that others be so.

However, what we learn via the news can be quite misleading in terms of the safety of a destination. Just because a country is in the news for danger doesn't mean that it is dangerous everywhere. If you want to go to a place that's on the wrong side of safe according to the media, I recommend the following:

Tips for Choosing a Safe Destination

- Check with your government's website for travel warnings. Be aware that government warnings tend to be very broad geographically and they can be out of date as they have a greater urgency to put up a warning than to take it down.
- Go to the Solo Travel Society on Facebook (facebook.com/solotravelsociety) and ask about your destination. See if you can find current or recent travelers in the area.
- Go on Twitter and ask for people's perspectives on your destination. Feel free to tweet me (@solotraveler) your question and I will retweet it for my followers.
- Contact the tourist board for your destination. They certainly want you to come but they also want you to be safe. They don't want to damage their reputation. They want good stories from their destination and should dissuade you if there is a problem.
- Look at sites such as Lonely Planet's Thorn Tree travel forum or BootsnAll's destination forums. Both can offer current information from travelers and expatriates in the area.
- Use information from people and organizations in the know about your specific destination to inform your decision.
- Take into consideration the sources of your information, balance all that you hear and then listen to yourself. If you are not confident, don't go.

At your destination there will also be some places that are safer than others. Experienced solo travelers know instinctively when a place is safe and when it isn't. But new solo travelers may not be so naturally astute. Here are a few generalizations to give you an idea of how to assess a location for its safety.

Knowing what's safe

What's safe is easier than what is not, so we'll start here.

- Places where families go tend to be safe: zoos, amusement parks or aquariums. If it is designed for and attracts families, it is likely safe.
- Typical tourist sites such as museums, churches and castles are safe.
- Well traveled hiking trails (if you see someone every 5 minutes or so) tend to be safe.
- Small towns, where everyone knows everyone, tend to be safe. They keep each other in check.
- Public spaces in cities such as markets, open parks, pubs in good areas and shopping districts are safe. In public we are naturally protected by social values. In private, we are subject to the values of those around us.

A safety helmet if necessary – Zugspitz Arena Alps, Austria.

Signals that a Place is Not Safe

Sometimes it's obvious when a place isn't safe. Other times, it's your "Spidey sense" that tingles and tells you to leave. Listen to it. Here, again, are some generalizations.

- Restaurants and other places near train stations are not unsafe in and of themselves but they are natural places for people to hang out who want to scam or pickpocket a tourist. If you need to go to a restaurant near a train or bus station, try inside the station itself or going a few blocks away.
- Remote areas for hiking or camping where there is no chance for help if required can be unsafe. Take extra precautions.
- There are areas in almost every town and city that are not safe and you can't always tell by the way they look. A nice looking neighborhood could have things going down that you don't know about. Likewise, what you consider dangerous-looking at home could be very safe in another country. Don't judge an area by the way it looks as much as by the people who are in it. If you think you may have entered an area that isn't quite right, leave. If you don't know how, choose a person carefully and ask for directions. If they want to take you, it may feel like the right thing to do but, if it doesn't, don't hesitate to decline the support.

The Ultimate Safe Place for Solo Travelers

When traveling alone – going to safe places, avoiding unsafe ones – it's important to remember that the place you're staying is your most important safe place of all. Try to keep your accommodation location to yourself. Meeting new people while traveling solo is a wonderful experience but an evening is not enough time to know a person's character. Keep your hotel, B&B or hostel address to yourself so that it is always safe. And if asked directly where you're staying, answer in vague terms.

66 *Travel expands our sense of community. Beginning with my first international travel experience as a Grade 11 student when I broke away from our tour group and tried to explain to an elderly flower seller that I couldn't afford the lovely bouquet he offered – until I realized he was offering the flowers as a gift – I have understood that our 'community' is global and not just where we live. Travel, particularly traveling solo, enables us to be part of such magical moments of community and friendship.* 99

Kathy
50-something, Toronto, Canada

Sixty Tips for Solo Safety

You can't help it. No matter how you try to blend in, you will give yourself away in many ways, large and small. You are a traveler. A tourist. And because tourists are marks for some of the less genial of characters, please have a read of these tips. Many are just good common sense but, sometimes, they will offer common sense that you may not have considered.

They are organized by the four priorities of safety: your person, your documents, your money and your stuff.

Your Person
Before you Leave

- Choose a destination appropriate for your travel experience. If this is your first solo travel adventure, go someplace where you speak the language and the culture is familiar. Or, if you choose an unfamiliar language and culture, start out on an organized tour and travel solo once you have the lay of the land.
- Do your research and know the risks of your destination before you arrive. Check your government's travel advisories. Travel guides are valuable sources of information. The Lonely Planet website includes links to a select list of travel blogs like Solo Traveler and has an active traveler community called Thorn Tree where you can ask your specific travel questions.
- Register with your government as a citizen abroad if you're going far and for a while. You can do this on their website.
- Ensure that your accommodation is in a safe part of town. Check it out on sites like TripAdvisor.com and use Google Maps Street View (if available) to see what the area looks like around your accommodation.
- Know the visa requirements of your destination.
- When booking your transportation, schedule your arrival in a new location early in the day so that you have time to adapt to unexpected situations.
- Study city maps so that you have the lay of the land and are able to walk with confidence.

- If you are a quiet person, before leaving, take some time in your basement or some other appropriate place and practice yelling – loudly. We are trained to keep our voices down in public but there may be a time when you will need it.
- Ensure that your cell phone will work where you're traveling and add important phone numbers like those of your accommodation, emergency contacts, family members (with country codes) and your embassy.
- Buy travel insurance. It's a tedious but important detail.
- Schedule vaccinations if appropriate.

Stay Safe in Public
- Always stay in public. Public is always safer than private.
- Stay in well-lit, well-traveled places.
- Ask locals and other travelers about the safety of an area or destination. Be proactive and choose who you gather information from.
- Stay in touch with home on a regular basis.
- If you see someone suddenly in need of help, go find help for them. Don't go to their aid alone.
- Consider avoiding restaurants near train or bus stations where unsavory characters often look for vulnerable targets.
- When you see signs telling you to be careful of pickpockets, DON'T suddenly check for your valuables! It's a common reaction and pickpockets watch for people doing just that around these signs so that they know where to pick.
- Carry the name and address of the place you're staying in the local language on a card.
- Dress and act with modesty. Don't flash jewelry, equipment or gadgets of any kind. What you consider cheap could be worth a lot in another place.
- Watch and learn. Take pause before you walk into a public space or even pick up a tomato at a vegetable stand. You'll avoid going into places you shouldn't tread and discover what good manners are in that culture.
- Be aware of your surroundings, the location of exits, the people near you and landmarks to orient yourself.
- If you're a jogger, check about the safety of your route and know it well

before going for a run. Ask your guesthouse for recommendations to be sure your route is safe.

- Walk with confidence. Walk like you absolutely know what you're doing.
- Don't wear ear buds or headphones. It makes you unaware of what's going on around you and also makes you look like an easy mark.
- Let a trusted person know where you are going. Because hotel staff have shift changes, you might also leave a note in your room.
- Be aware of and use official taxis only. Official airport taxis are usually less expensive than regular taxis serving the airport. Rogue taxi drivers will serve in peak periods when it's difficult to get a regular cab, but they will charge you a premium and you don't have the protection of a licensed cab. If in doubt, go to a hotel and ask them to get you a cab. Do a bit of research on taxi etiquette at your destination before you leave. Know whether you can hail a cab and how to tell if a cab is available. Find out whether you get a car to yourself, or if they pick up multiple passengers. Also know if they should always run the meter, if you should bargain for your fare, or if there are flat rate options.
- Download maps of transit systems and study them before you set out so that you don't spend undue time studying them in the subway station. Learn the fare system and buy a transit pass available in most major cities. It will always be easier (and sometimes less expensive) to travel during off peak hours.
- Don't get on empty subway cars or ones with only a couple of people on them. Choose the busier cars.
- Ask for a hotel room on an upper floor. Women might ask if there is a women-only floor and get a room there if possible.
- Be aware of the alternative exits.
- When you return at night, ask for an escort to your room if you are nervous.
- Use the security lock.
- Carry a whistle to attract attention if you are in a dangerous situation.
- Don't take money out of your money belt, ever. It's there for safekeeping; your money for the day should be in your wallet.

View from the top of Mayan Pyramid, Tonino - a part of Mexico that is
quite safe in a country that is sometimes considered unsafe.

Stay Safe with Strangers (Still in Public)

- Trust your intuition. If a person or place doesn't feel right, leave. Be rude if necessary. Malcolm Gladwell studied the potential of an intuitive response in his book Blink: The Power of Thinking Without Thinking. It is powerful. Listen to your gut.
- Stay sober and well rested so that your intuition and decision-making are optimal.
- Keep where you're staying to yourself. Your accommodation should be your safe haven.
- Don't be rushed into making a decision, whether it's a purchase, transportation or accommodation. If you feel rushed you won't be thinking clearly. Find a way to take pause. You can count to 50, do 60 seconds of mindful meditation or simply think of an image that calms you.
- Adapt to and respect cultural differences. Be polite on your host country's terms as well as your own.

A Message to Young Solo Travelers

66 *When traveling solo, your first responsibility is to be safe. If this means losing your money, missing an opportunity, acting rude or selfish, go for it.* 99

Your Documents

- Keep your passport and other important documents in the same, secure place at all times. Your passport may stay on you but your trip insurance may stay in your backpack. Wherever you choose, be consistent throughout the trip, and on all trips, and you will be less likely to lose them.
- Have photocopies of your documents with you and have electronic backups as well. You can scan and e-mail your documents to yourself or use one of a number of online document storage services. Also leave copies with a family member or friend at home.

Your Money

- Read the "Managing Money" part of Section 2.
- If you want to carry a purse, it should be one with a long, strong strap. Wear it across your shoulder with the opening against your body. This strategy foiled a scooter bandit in Naples, Italy who got away with nothing when trying to rob me.
- Carry small amounts of cash in your wallet but have more available in a more discreet place.
- Consider pre-paid debit cards. Some experts consider them better in terms of protecting your personal information than credit cards.
- Only have one credit card accessible. Store the other in a discreet place.
- Traveler's checks may be a good backup if you lose money in North America or Europe and can get to a bank. They are not as useful in other parts of the world.

Your Stuff

- Lock your room carefully and lock important items in the room safe. If there is no safe or locker, lock valuables inside your main luggage when you are out.
- Choose hostels that offer lockers or secure places for luggage. If it doesn't look safe, don't leave your most valuable items, or ask the front desk if they have a safe.
- Minimize the number of enticing items you carry.
- Don't wear jewelry or flash expensive technology.

- Know what really matters to you. I have a three-point check: my wallet, my passport and my camera. Those are the three things that really matter to me.
- If you use a daypack, carry it on your front with the opening against your body when in busy areas and/or attach a twist tie or Velcro to keep the zippers together.
- Use a shopping bag from a local store to minimize the tourist look.
- When you leave your room, leave the TV and a light on if possible and put out the 'do not disturb' sign.

Technology as a Safety Tool

- Load your cell phone with all important numbers at home and at your destination and enable a password lockout function.
- Keep your cell phone handy so that you can call for help if necessary.
- If your phone has a siren, learn how to use it. If not, download one from the iTunes store.
- Download a GPS and a translator to your phone.

The Beautiful Children of Jordan

"What's your name?"

"What's your name?"

> "Janice."

"Ah, beautiful. Beautiful."

> "What's your name?"

"Jasmine."

"Farah."

"Halah."

"Raniyah."

There were so many names and so many beautiful, exuberant, outgoing girls on school excursions to Jerash the day I was there.

They wanted to take my picture. They wanted me to take theirs. They wanted to know my name and for me to know theirs. Mostly, they just wanted to talk to a woman who was obviously a foreigner, practice their English which they start learning in grade one, and have fun!

The children I met in Jerash were open, friendly, confident, curious and boisterous. They freely came up and asked me questions, sometimes bouncing up in front of my face to get my attention in a crowd. I loved it.

One teacher told me that the children were thrilled that I was chatting with them as other tourists had ignored them earlier in the day. What a shame. In a land with Petra, Wadi Rum, the Red Sea and the Dead Sea — in a country with so much to offer — these children were, without a doubt, the highlight of my trip. Regardless of what a country has for travelers, in my estimation, it is the people that make the trip. Jordan is a destination worth revisiting.

The children of Jordan were a joy – Jeresh, Jordan.

Safe Answers to Common Questions

Some people put up a shield when they travel solo by wearing a wedding ring or carrying a picture of a brother to substitute for a husband. But, I'm a really bad liar. So, instead, I've developed the ability to answer common questions with truthful, vague and safe answers. Here are a few examples...

Where are you staying?

Answer: At a B&B in the ____ district. (The answer is not evasive but not specific. You can also elaborate about how the owner has taken you under their wing.)

Can I drive/walk you to your hotel?

Answer: Thanks, but I've already called a taxi. (Take a bathroom run and call a taxi before new friends are making a move to leave. That way you can honestly express gratitude but not accept the ride. In a private car you no longer have control.) If you are in a place where there are no taxis, say that you're not looking to leave as yet.

Are you really traveling alone?

Answer: Yes and no. I always have someone looking out for me. OR, Yes, but I'm expecting my friend to arrive this evening. (Give people the impression that should you go missing for a minute, people would know.)

What are you up to this evening?

Answer: I have plans. (To spend the evening without this person, keep your response as vague as that. If you wouldn't mind spending the evening with them, meet in a public place away from your accommodation and return via taxi.)

How old are you? (or some more subtle variation)

Answer: Old enough not to tell you. (ha, ha, ha) (Young and older travelers can be targets for con artists whereas people in their 30s, 40s or 50s are less so. Try to present yourself in this age range.)

Recognize Potential Danger

An ounce of prevention...you've heard the adage. In this case, it is really important. Preventing a dangerous situation is far easier than defusing one.

Read the Obvious Red Flags

Being aware of your surroundings and how people are acting is critical to your safety.

- Recognize the signs of a bad area. Judge an area by the people there, not the state of the buildings. This is a difficult issue for generalizations because what looks 'bad' at home may be typical in another country. Closed stores, few people, or no families wandering around can be indicators of an area you want to leave.
- Watch for signs of an unsavory person: contradictions in their story, difficulty maintaining eye contact or making inappropriate demands.
- Look out for services that don't look legitimate: unofficial accommodation offers, unlicensed taxis or someone offering to change money at a great rate.

Know the Common Scams Before you Travel

Watch out for people:

- Posing as police, showing fake ID and asking to see your wallet for counterfeit currency. Scam.
- Telling you an attraction is closed today, but they will take you somewhere else.

- Giving you something apparently free and then demanding payment. They can be very difficult to say no to, but you must. They'll demand payment as soon as the item is in your hands.
- Taking your picture for you and then demanding a fee.
- Spilling ice cream, ketchup or coffee on you or causing some other distraction so that their partner can pick your pocket.
- Managing your credit card while on the phone. A cashier doing this may be taking a photo of your card with the phone's camera.
- Operating the China tea scam – inviting you to tea and leaving you with an enormous bill. Very different than the genuine offers of tea you'll get in, say, India.

Across Canada By Train

While Canada is known for its expansive territory in the north, almost 90% of Canadians live within sixty miles of the American border. Canada is essentially an east–west country. Sitting in central Canada planning a spring train trip, I had two choices: go east, or go west. With family in Vancouver, I chose west.

For this trip, I chose to travel coach. I did so for two reasons: the price and the people – the latter being the most important. In first class there are many very nice people but in coach, there are really interesting people. On my trip to Vancouver, I spent three days (and three nights) with the most interesting, entertaining people one could imagine. It started before leaving the station.

The Casket Makers
I boarded the train, organized my stuff, sat down and looked across the aisle. There sat a young teenage boy with a wooden casket for a suitcase.

"Yes," I thought. "This is going to be an interesting trip."

Shortly after we pulled out of the station I could contain myself no longer. "Uh, what's that?" I asked.

The boy was about 13 and still in the sweet boy stage. "It's a model casket," he said. "My Dad and I make pine boxes."

"Ahhh," I said.

When his Dad returned I got the full story. Father and son were from Prince George, British Columbia and makers of simple pine boxes. They had taken the train from Prince George to Toronto to be on the television show, The Dragon's Den – a reality show where you pitch your company to get financing from five successful business people. The pitch hadn't won them any money but it had been an adventure and had gained publicity for their company.

Having recently experienced far too much death in my own family, I had a very interesting discussion with the father.

Burning Man Survivors

The bar car on a train is like a kids' playground. You just have to watch for a bit, wait for an opening and jump in. This may not work in your neighborhood bar, but on the train it's almost expected. There is no established social order. Everyone is traveling. And everyone has a tale to tell.

It was in the bar car that I met a wonderful, aging hippie couple from – well, from nowhere any more. They used to have a home in Manitoba but they sold that and chose travel instead. To have some sort of base they had recently bought a share in a trailer in northern Manitoba. This couple told of their journeys. The one that stands out most in my mind was their experience at Burning Man, an annual art event/temporary community built in the Nevada desert. They were the first people I had ever met who had a firsthand account of this legendary event.

Multicultural Euchre

I like the options that trains offer. Heading out west, when I felt like solitude, I spent time at my seat reading or watching the scenery. When I wanted fun, I just went to the dome car where I could get a better view of the landscape and socialize.

Most people on the train were from various provinces in Canada but I also met people from Korea, France, Germany and Japan. Walking into the dome car at one point, an adult was leaving a kids' game of euchre. They needed a fourth – adults tire of such games faster than kids. I joined in. Four players from three countries. We had a great time.

And Many Others...

In addition to these highlights there was the guy from Israel who told me all about the love of his life, the couple from Newfoundland who had been sleeping side by side in coach for four days en route to see a new grandchild, the retired railroad worker who explained how the train signals worked across the prairies and the fellow from Quebec who was the first of his family to travel outside of the province.

Canada is a spectacular country and traveling by train is a great way to see it. It takes time but it is well worth it.

"The Canadian" goes from Toronto to Vancouver – Via Rail across Canada.

Happy Trails - Bon Voyage - Safe Travels

Remember the couch I wrote about in the Back Story?

Well, since launching Solo Traveler, my relationship with it has changed dramatically. It is now a place for dreaming, not grieving. When I got up off the couch that Saturday afternoon, my life was different.

Two months later, I launched Solo Traveler. Six weeks after that I was on my first trip as a blogger. Now, three years and many trips later, I find daily joy in the comments left on my blog, in Twitter exchanges and in discussions on a Facebook community ironically named The Solo Travel Society. I enjoy meeting other solo travelers wherever I go and I love speaking about the entire experience to groups.

I've been rehearsing for this role my entire life.
It has been said to me:

> "Yes, it's easy for you. You're an extrovert."

In fact, I'm not. Speak to those who knew me in my teens and twenties and they'll tell you that I was shy. Talk to anyone who was in the audience the one time that I stood at a podium in my thirties and they'll tell you that it was a painful experience for the entire room. No, it's not that I'm outgoing; it's that I'm willing to go out and try. And, the more I've done it, the more experience I've accumulated, the more extraordinary my travel has become.

And now it's your turn.
I think I've shared most of what I wanted to say now. I've given you tips about money and packing, road trips and long-term travel, safety and meeting people. While there is much more about solo travel on my blog, really, what's left is for you to go.

Yes, go. Go around the world or around the corner. Go solo and enjoy the people, culture, history, mountain views, seascapes and city skylines. Enjoy adventures and challenges.

But, mostly, go and enjoy how solo travel enriches your life. Discover the world as you discover yourself.

Go and see what you don't know is there.

RESOURCES

Resources

Accommodation
AirBnB.com
BedandBreakfast.com
CouchSurfing.org
Flipkey.com
HomeAway.com
HouseTrip.com
Hostelbookers.com
Hostelworld.com

Books
The Career Break Traveler's Handbook
The Food Traveler's Handbook
The Luxury Traveler's Handbook
The Volunteer Traveler's Handbook

Budgeting and Money Management
BudgetYourTrip.com - Has basic cost information on a variety of destinations.
ThePointsGuy.com - How to get the most out of loyalty programs.
TravelHacking.org - a service that helps you with travel hacking.
Xpenser.com - An expense tracker and management tool.

Connecting with Locals and other Travelers
CouchSurfing.org - Many people use CouchSurfing.org as a means of connecting with locals even if they are not using couch surfing for accommodation.
Hermail.net - An international directory of women travelers.
Meetup.com - Find groups that share your interests (food, politics, wine, knitting, architecture, etc.) and are holding meetings in your destination city.
Trekkingpartners.com - Find partners to trek and hike all over the world.
WomenWelcomeWomen.org.uk - 5W is a network of about 2,400 women in over 80 countries ready to help other women with their travels.

Find Great Dining Experiences

Chowhound.com - A community for foodies with discussions sorted by location. This is a great resource for finding foodies' favorite restaurants in most major cities.

FoodbyCountry.com - A little bit of history, an overview of food and some recipes.

GlobalTableAdventure.com - Travel, food, photos and recipes.

Legalnomads.com - Blog by the author of The Food Traveler's Handbook.

Long-Term Travel

CareerBreakSecrets.com - An inspiring career break blog offering lots of long-term travel tips.

GoBackpacking.com - Practical, budget-oriented travel advice for planning your own trips.

MeetPlanGo.com - Annual meetings to inspire long-term travel and answer questions of those wanting to go, plus Career Break Basic Training online.

WanderingEarl.com - Earl is a travel blogger who has been on the road since 1999. Great insights.

Solo Travel Resources

SoloFriendly.com - A blog for solo travelers that focuses primarily on American destinations.

SoloTravelerBlog.com - Solo Traveler is the blog for those who travel alone by author Janice Waugh.

SoloTravelerBlog.com/deals - This page on Solo Traveler focuses on special deals that don't have a single supplement.

Staying Connected

TravelBlog.org - Free personal travel blog tool.

TravelPod.com - Free personal travel blog tool.

Blogger.com - Free blogging platform.

WordPress.com - Free blogging platform.

Tumblr.com - Free short-form, easy to use blogging tool.

Google Voice - Good option for Americans.

Skype - Good option for all.

Travel Forums

Boards.bootsnall.com - Boots 'n All

Facebook.com/solotravelsociety - The Solo Travel Society is connected to Solo Traveler.

Fodors.com/community - Fodor's travel forum.

Lonelyplanet.com/thorntree - Thorntree on Lonely Planet

Tripadvisor.com - Search the site for Solo Travel Forum for excellent discussions.

Useful tools

Airninja.com - Flight search.

Expedia.com - Flight search.

Maps.Google.com/streetview - A tool for checking out a neighborhood before you go.

Hipmunk.com - Flight search.

iTunes - there are hundreds of free apps for translation, maps and travel information.

Oanda.com - Currency conversion tool

Orbitz.com - Flight search.

SitorSquat.com - Tells you where the nearest bathrooms are and what they're like.

TripAdvisor.com - Travelers' reviews of accommodation and more. (To be taken with a grain of salt as reviews can be planted.)

Tripit - Manages your basic travel information in one place.

Janice Waugh

Janice Waugh publishes Solo Traveler [solotravelerblog.com], the blog for those who travel alone. She has been quoted in many media outlets including CNN, the Washington Post, the Chicago Tribune, the Los Angeles Times and the Toronto Star. In addition to writing, she enjoys speaking to groups about solo travel and was thrilled to be invited to do so at the Smithsonian in Washington, D.C. Her blog offers solo travel stories, tips, safety advice and destination ideas. *The Solo Traveler's Handbook* was first published in 2011. This 2nd edition is published concurrently with four other guides on the "how" and "why" of travel. Collectively, they form a series called The Traveler's Handbooks. Janice has a Master's Degree in History. When not traveling, she lives in Toronto.

Janice Waugh

Janice Waugh